A SHORT INTRODUCTION TO ETHICS

Gerald J. Williams

University Press of America,® Inc.
Lanham • New York • Oxford

Copyright © 1999
University Press of America,® Inc.
4720 Boston Way
Lanham, Maryland 20706

12 Hid's Copse Rd.
Cumnor Hill, Oxford OX2 9JJ

All rights reserved
Printed in the United States of America
British Library Cataloging in Publication Information Available

Library of Congress Cataloging-in-Publication Data

Williams, Gerald J.
A short introduction to ethics / Gerald J. Williams
p.   cm.
Includes bibliographical references and index.
l. Ethics. I. Title.
BJ1025.W47   1998   170—dc21   98-47984 CIP

ISBN 0-7618-1301-2 (pbk: alk. ppr.)

for Ann

A. M. D. G.

Contents

Preface

I have become convinced, after many years of teaching a variety of courses in ethics, that a short volume written in a reasonably straightforward and somewhat relaxed, even conversational, style would help students prepare for the in-depth study of the questions, issues, and puzzles they have to deal with in standard ethics or moral philosophy courses. It is my hope that *A Short Introduction to Ethics* meets this objective.

Early chapters deal with some of what I like to call the "puzzles" of moral philosophy, e.g., selecting the features of an action that are appropriate for deciding whether it's morally right or wrong; how the difficulties of weighing and foreseeing consequences affect moral decision-making; how freedom and knowledge enter into pinpointing moral responsibility; whether the notion of moral knowledge makes any sense; whether it is correct to distinguish between causal and moral responsibility. I then discuss cultural moral relativism and three moral theories: utilitarianism, natural law, and Kant's pure practical reason emphasizing the fundamental dichotomy between consequentialism and nonconsequentialism expressed in the idea that there are actions that are intrinsically wrong and are absolutely forbidden-no matter what kind or how many good consequences they might produce.

The chapter on natural law is, I believe, treated in substantially more detail than it receives in many ethics textbooks, an approach that may clarify the philosophical thinking underlying much of the current controversy over issues like abortion, assisted suicide and euthanasia, artificial contraception, cloning, sterilization, homosexuality, the use of condoms to prevent AIDS, surrogate motherhood, and the use of -in-vitro fertilization to overcome sterility.

Chapter 9 deals in considerable detail with the definition and source of human rights.

Chapter 10 considers the nature of a *moral* virtue, e.g., whether all "excellences" or good qualities should be regarded as moral virtues. I also address the controversy over whether virtue ethics or moral theory is the correct way to think about and live the moral life.

Although I had students in mind when I prepared this book, the general reader interested in what moral philosophy is all about may also find it useful.

Gerald J. Williams

Acknowledgments

My sincere thanks to David O'Connor, Vicente Medina, Albert Hakim, John Ranieri and William Smith, all of Seton Hall University; to Andrew Rubino, a graduate of Seton Hall, and to Mervyn D'Souza of Kean University for their helpful comments, criticisms, and suggestions. My heartfelt appreciation to Msgr. Paul J. Hayes for the valuable insights he provided during our many discussions of natural law. I am especially grateful to our daughter, Helen Zubaly, for her invaluable editorial assistance. Finally, my thanks to Helen Hudson, University Press of America's production editor, for her prompt and professional help in getting this book to press.

Chapter 1

Deciding What's Morally Permissible

Some Hard Questions

When is it morally permissible to kill another human being? In a war to defend our country? In self-defense against a murderous attacker? When we execute murderers?

Is it ever right to deliberately inflict pain on someone? Should the police torture a terrorist who won't tell where he's planted a bomb that is going to kill innocent people when it explodes?

Is it morally legitimate for someone in emotional despair or in intolerable physical pain caused by a debilitating disease to commit suicide? Would it be all right to help that person do it?

What do we do with newborns who are severely disabled, mentally or physically? Should they be allowed to die? Would it be better to kill them, mercifully, in order to spare them what many think would be a miserable and intolerable existence?

Is sex outside marriage morally licit? Is marriage for life, or are there times when a divorce is better for spouses and children?

Should a society tolerate homosexual lifestyles?

Are abortion, sterilization, artificial contraception, surrogate motherhood and cloning of human beings ever morally right?

Is democracy really the best form of government? Where does the authority of the state come from? What laws of our state or country should we obey and why? May we disobey our country's laws selectively; i.e., may we engage in civil disobedience or fudge on our taxes to avoid supporting government programs we don't agree with?

Are we always obliged to serve in our country's armed forces? What if we think our country is fighting an unjust war? May we be selective conscientious objectors choosing, on moral grounds, those wars we will or won't fight in?

Are our government agencies always morally correct in what they do just because they are "the government?"   Should those agencies concerned with our international relations ever assassinate leaders of other countries or subvert our laws and constitution if they think that's in our country's best interests?

Is discrimination in housing, employment, or service in political office on grounds of race, gender, sexual preference, handicapped status, age, weight or ethnic origin justified if that's what the local or national culture demands?

May we keep people out of our country just because of their color or ethnic origins?

Is it just for one level of society to live very well while other members of that same society don't have enough resources to live decent human lives?

Do we have a moral obligation to provide economic and other kinds of assistance to poor and underdeveloped countries?

How should we treat animals? Since they are conscious beings, do they have rights? May we kill them for sport or eat them?

Consider the world of business. Are there actions people in business might have to do for what seems to be the good of their companies or communities but wouldn't think of doing in their private lives? Could preserving jobs, bolstering a community's economy, or preserving the value of shareholders' equity justify lying on time sheets or expense accounts; fudging the company's books; telling lies in advertising copy; continuing to sell a product that is seriously harmful to some or a great many of its users; publishing pornography; falsifying information on bids to win a contract or dumping toxic wastes where they might harm a community's water supply?

How Do We Answer These Questions?

How do we go about answering these questions? How do we make the moral judgments of right and wrong they call for? Ordinarily, we appeal to the moral principles, the beliefs we hold about what is morally right or wrong. These beliefs may come from our ethnic traditions, our cultural practices, our religion; or they may come from a moral theory. Each of these sources must, of course, establish its credentials, show the legitimacy of its claim to be a guide to making moral choices. In this book, I'll be concerned with just one of them: moral theory.

Moral Theory

Very simply put, a theory is a systematic study of a particular subject matter, including the assumptions, principles and procedures needed to understand it thoroughly. Philosophers who reflect systematically on the moral questions and conflicts arising out of the conditions and experience of human life propose moral theories, i.e., rationales, for a principle or set of principles used to determine whether an action is morally right or wrong, to be done or avoided. In effect, they try to establish a standard for making moral judgments, Philosophers who claim that their standard is universal and unchanging, applying everywhere to everyone, are moral *objectivists* or moral *absolutists*. (Some philosophers use the word "absolutist" to indicate a theory that claims that at least some moral principles permit no exceptions to what they prescribe.) Other philosophers, moral *relativists*, conclude that there is no such universal standard, that moral choices are simply relative to what individuals or societies believe about them.

Virtue

Some philosophers argue that morality is really a question of virtuous conduct, that we must acquire good moral habits, develop a good moral character. A few of them believe that engaging in endless and seemingly irresolvable debates about the grounds for determining why actions are morally right or wrong, whether, e.g., the consequences of an action or some other feature like motive and circumstances or some special consideration offered by reason are what are relevant to making moral judgments, does not address what leading a moral life is all about.

In this book, I will use the traditional approach of considering what philosophers have had to say about moral theory, but I'll treat the question of virtue as well. My own belief is that neither way of "doing ethics" is sufficient by itself, that both need to be considered in any complete account of moral philosophy.

Moral Theory: Who Needs It?

Why should we be concerned about moral theory anyway? One simple answer is that our own well-being and that of others depends on our making informed moral judgments.   How we make those everyday moral decisions, assuming we don't just make them mindlessly, depends, I believe, on the moral thinking we subscribe to. One of the jobs of moral philosophers is to examine and analyze the many approaches to making moral judgments to see whether they are reasonable, whether the rationales that have been used to lay down rules of conduct are sound, and to pass the results of that study on to the rest of us by formal courses, books, articles and discussions so that we can think through our own ideas about morality and decide whether we're comfortable with them or might want to modify or even change them.

That's what this book is all about: providing some basic understanding of what moral philosophers do.   I won't attempt to answer all those question I teased you with earlier; rather, I hope to help you understand some of the fundamental issues dealt with in the study of moral philosophy, or ethics, so that you will be better prepared to pursue that study in some depth, if you so choose.   The book may even help you make your own moral judgments on a more reasoned, more principled basis when you are confronted with conflicts in your life that call for moral decisions.

What Are We Talking About? Moral Terms

The study of any subject matter requires an understanding of the terms used to define, describe, and analyze it.   The following are definitions of just a few of the basic terms used in this book and any course or book on ethics.   These definitions are offered now to help you begin to understand what we're saying when we talk about ethics. Other terms will be defined as they come up in subsequent chapters.
ꞑ *Ethics*:   rules and standards telling members of a community, or profession how they ought to behave. A *code of ethics*

consists of actions prescribed or prohibited according to some moral standard or rule as set out by some society or organization for its members. The term also refers to the formal study of moral issues: e.g., moral principles and the standards on which they are based, how moral judgments are made, and the meaning of moral language. "Ethics" and "moral philosophy" are often used interchangeably in this context.

o *Morality:* A system of rules of conduct.

o *Moral theory:* a systematic proposal of a standard, a rationale, reasons for judging whether actions are morally right or wrong.

o *"Right" and "wrong:"* words used to describe actions that conform or don't conform to a moral standard. Actions are also described by words like good, righteous, praiseworthy, decent, generous, bad, heinous, callous, and selfish. For my purposes, I'll use "right" and "wrong" to describe actions that are judged morally allowed or forbidden according to a particular moral theory.

o *Moralist:* one who studies and perhaps teaches, theorizes, and writes about moral issues. In this book, I will use the terms "moral philosopher" and "moral theorist" interchangeably with this term.

o *Moral relativism:* the idea that there is no one standard of moral behavior applicable to everyone all the time. Actions are judged right or wrong relative to a society's or individual's code of behavior.

o *Cultural relativism:* the idea that actions are judged right or wrong according to whether they conform or not to a particular society's code or mores.

o *Moral subjectivism:* an extreme version of moral relativism: the idea that actions are right or wrong according to each individual's code of behavior.

o *Moral absolutism:* the idea that there is one universal standard of moral behavior. The term is also used by some moral philosophers to indicate that there are no exceptions to at least some moral principles.

o *Moral principle:* a rule or generalization about a kind of action, e.g., "never murder," "don't steal," or "don't lie."

o *Consequentialism* (teleology): the idea that the ultimate grounds for judging an action right or wrong are the good and bad non-moral effects or state of affairs it produces for another person or persons.

o *Nonconsequentialism* (deontology): the idea that consequences are not the ultimate grounds for determining right and wrong; God's

commandments, duty, or certain rules developed by reason are.
o *Permissible:* what we are allowed to do, morally speaking.
o *Impermissible:* what we are *not* allowed to do, morally speaking.
o *Conscience:* an awareness of, a judgment that what we are about to do is morally permissible or impermissible, that we should or should not do it.
o *Virtue:* moral goodness, excellence.

Making It Easy

For ease of reading, I have not used footnotes in the main text to indicate the source of material from the philosophers whose ideas I talk about. You will find their works listed as appropriate by chapter in an appendix titled: "Sources." Another appendix, "Resources," contains a bibliography of some standard textbooks, other books on the general topic of ethics, and articles that may be of interest should you want to pursue your study of ethics further.

Chapter 2

What Counts in Judging the Moral Character of An Action?

Moral Judgments

Simply put, ethics is about what we ought to do or ought not to do, so one fundamental task of moral philosophy is to think about how to decide whether actions are morally right or wrong, i.e, how to make moral judgments.

Note that "right" and "wrong" are technical terms commonly used by professional moralists; other descriptions that are useful in characterizing actions include words like good, decent, generous, praiseworthy, bad, callous, heinous, and shameful. For my purposes, I'll use "right" and "wrong" to cover the essential thrust of what making moral decisions is all about.

There are two ways to look at these judgments. One is what we might call "subjective," the evaluation made by the individual performing an act, the agent; how he or she sees it and decides whether it is morally all right to do it. The other is "objective," the appraisal made from the perspective of a neutral observer who applies an objective moral standard of some kind or brings some peculiar view about morality to an action but is not involved in it.

I prefer, for my purposes, to use the objective approach in what follows in order to bring into sharper focus those features of actions that are relevant to making moral judgments about them, all the while acknowledging that individuals act and judge what they do from their own perspectives, according to their own consciences.

How actions are described, which of their features are selected for evaluating them morally or for forming moral principles understood as generalizations about actions or as "rules of action" (e.g., "never commit murder"), is crucial.   As we'll see later, different moral theorists select different features as the essential elements for moral assessment and, as a result, often come up with different conclusions about the very same act.

Let's examine two scenarios to illustrate what I mean by an action's "features."

The Self-defense Scenario

Suppose a woman shot and killed her estranged husband who assaulted her and who, she believed, intended to kill her. What is it about her act that needs to be considered in order to decide whether she did something morally right or wrong? Consider:
o Is it just the fact that she killed a human being?
o Does the fact that the attack was unjust make it all right for her to kill her assailant outright, or do we need to ask whether she used more force than necessary to stop him?
o Would it make more sense to consider her husband's death morally irrelevant in this situation and concentrate solely on what her motive was, i.e., her desire to save her life?
o Should only the results of her action count, the consequences, so that the act itself of killing and what she wanted to accomplish, her motive, are irrelevant as long as the overall outcome of what she did was good?
o What went on in her head, what beliefs did she have before she shot her husband?

This last point requires a little elaboration. What I mean here is what goes on in a person's mind before he or she "does something," acts overtly (publicly, openly, in a way others can observe): i.e., deliberating over options, choosing or deciding, and intending.   I believe that a person can act "in his or her head," as it were, without doing anything publicly observable and may even do something right or wrong without ever showing any visible behavior. I would do something wrong, for instance, if I were to think to myself knowingly, willingly, and intentionally, without every telling anyone what I was thinking: "I hate that man, and I hope something terrible happens to him." Or, think about a man who is tempted to steal something in a store but decides not to.   It doesn't seem strange to count that as an "action." If he told us that he had decided not to do something morally wrong, it would be perfectly natural to praise him for his decision, for "what he did."

Based then, on what we've considered so far in the case where the woman shot her husband, it appears correct to say that an action's features include a basic description of it, without necessarily giving it a moral quality (e.g., "killing"); deliberation; choice or decision, and motive as well as circumstances (the situation) and a state of affairs or consequences the action produces. The challenge for moral theorists is to decide which of these are essential for judging that an action is morally right or wrong. Let's examine the case in more detail to see what might count in making that decision.

The Action: What's Happening

The description of what the woman did appropriately includes the fact that she shot and killed her husband. If killing another human being is considered wrong in itself regardless of the situation in which it is done, then clearly nothing else is needed to decide that she did something morally wrong. Few moralists, I believe, are willing to believe that killing, in itself, is morally wrong, so we really need to know a lot more about her act to give it a proper moral description.

Deliberation, Decision, Circumstances (the Situation)

It's probably unlikely but possible that the woman didn't make a decision in the usual sense of that word; her action may have been purely reflexive--like throwing your arm up in front of your face if someone strikes out at you. In the case of purely reflexive actions over which we believe we have no control, deliberation, choosing, and deciding are absent, so it doesn't seem to make any sense to even try to make a moral judgment about them (I'm not talking about those reflexes we deliberately cultivate in order to practice some skill or art. We are, just because we have developed such reflexes, morally responsible for the actions that stem from them.)

Suppose, as would be more likely, that the woman in our case had had time to think about what was happening and deliberate about how she would choose to defend herself. Her perception of the situation might have included:

o The attack was unjust, which means she didn't kill an innocent person, i.e., she didn't commit murder.

o Her belief that she wasn't physically strong enough to disarm her attacker, so the only way to save herself was to use a gun.

o The fact that she was not an expert with this weapon and wasn't able to merely wound her husband, using just enough force to disable but not kill him.

Intention and Motive

The words "intention" and "motive" are frequently used synonomously, although it can be argued that they are really different from each other. When we do something, we design a plan of action that will produce the results, the state of affairs, the consequences we *want*. Our belief about what will result from that plan of action is part of our practical reasoning: to bring about the results we desire, we decide to act on that belief, we form an *intention* to act in the way that will accomplish them.

Now, in some cases, our belief about what an action will accomplish (and our intent to act on that belief) often covers the same ground that our desire does. But what if we believe that an action will bring about more consequences than we might want it to. Does that mean we also intend those further consequences if we proceed with the action? Do we intend *everything* our actions will produce--even if we don't *want* all they will cause? Is it possible to intend something to happen as part of a plan of action without wanting it to? Let's try to focus on this puzzle using the case we're pondering.

What did the woman *want* to do? What was the purpose of her action? Did she simply want to stop her husband's attack or did she want to kill him? It's obvious, of course, that she caused his death. Does that mean that even though his death might not have been what she wanted, it still has to be considered part of her *intention* because she could *foresee* that she might kill him, she knew what her action might accomplish over and above just stopping his attack?

It seems like his death should be considered part of her intention, since making a decision to carry out an action is forming an intention to do it, and that seems to include causing the consequences the agent knows will be associated with it. If, then, the act produces evil consequences as well as good ones, even though they weren't **wanted,** could those evil consequences ever be such that they might make the action evil and morally wrong--whatever the motive for doing it?

Let's look at this puzzle from another angle: just from the consideration of consequences alone, without reference to motive.

Consequences

What consequences of her action is the woman in our case responsible for? Everything that results, both directly and indirectly, from what she did? Let's speculate a little about some of the possible good and bad results of her action:

o Her children, should she have them, don't lose their mother.

o Whatever benefits her lifework offers society are preserved.

o Her friends and relatives are not deprived of her presence.

o Another person, her attacker, is dead.

o The assailant's children, should he have them, are left without their father.

o Society is denied the contribution of his lifework or, if he is a criminal, preserved from further harm he may cause.

o The husband's friends and other relatives may be afflicted with grief over his death.

o Etc., etc.

Note the "etc., etc." Where does it all stop? How far out in the future is she obliged to look when considering the consequences of her action? What about any bad consequences she can't foresee but is *causally* responsible for? That seems, on its face, to be absurd: how could people ever act on anything of any importance if they thought they would be held morally responsible for everything bad their actions might cause--no matter how remote and, especially, if they didn't know what they might be causing?

One answer might be that she must consider just what she can reasonably foresee. Even so, when do even the reasonably foreseen consequences she may cause begin to have a bearing on her moral responsibility? How does she decide where that point is? Does it begin just after the set of consequences she consciously wants to cause--for herself, say, and her loved ones? Would it ever make sense to say that while she is causally responsible for whatever bad consequences her action produces, she is morally blameless as long as the good consequences outweigh the bad ones?

The Bomb-Scare Scenario

Consider a second scenario. Imagine that you are in a room with three other people. Someone has installed, in the ceiling, an explosive device set to go off in two minutes. The bomber informs you that she has wired the device to the room's light switch so that you can disarm the bomb by pushing the switch to the "off" position. However, she also lets you know that if you do push the switch, it will detonate explosive devices in other parts of the building and will kill fifty or more people. May you push it? It's most likely true that all you *want* to do is to save your own and your companions' lives; you don't *mean* to kill the others. Does that relieve you of moral responsibility for their deaths if you push the switch--especially since you *know* they'll be killed?

Is Motive Totally Irrelevant?

Maybe motive is morally irrelevant when making moral judgments and all that really counts are the consequences of your action for yourself and all the others involved. But if only consequences count, why can't you consider just the consequences for yourself and perhaps the people in the room with you? Do you have to weigh your own and your companions' lives against the others' lives? Why isn't it simply a case of you or them? Does just the sheer number of people involved somehow make a difference? What if you and the other people in your room are highly-trained scientists working on a cure for AIDS or cancer? What if some of the fifty people in the other room are those scientists and you and your companions aren't? Is that enough to override the interest you have in your own life and the lives of the others with you in your room?

Or, *since you can't possibly know all the consequences* that will result from killing the people in the other parts of the building, something worse, perhaps, than just the deaths of you and the others with you, does that fact alone keep you from blowing them up?

Are Numbers Important?

Are numbers really important here? If so, just how do they apply? Is it simply the total number of lives in your room weighed against the total number of lives in the rest of the building? Perhaps numbers don't count at all. Maybe each individual's life interests-including what that life means to loved ones and society should be weighed against the interests and meaning of every other individual's life. If no one life has interests more significant on the whole than your own, why wouldn't you be justified in killing all the others as long as you own life was saved?

Causal and Moral Responsibility Distinguished

We do seem to hold people *causally* responsible for whatever effects they know their actions will produce. As you can now see from the puzzles we've just discussed that arise from considerations of consequences, the problem is whether people should be praised or blamed, *morally speaking,* for all of the states of affairs they know their actions will produce or just for those they *want.* We'll see later how different moral theories handle this challenge.

Chapter 3

When Are We Morally Responsible for What We Do?

Acting Knowingly and Willingly

When are we morally responsible for our actions? When should we be blamed or praised for what we have done? The most fundamental conditions for attributing moral responsibility to people seem to be that they *know* what they are doing and that they are doing what they do *freely,* without any external or internal compulsion.

Knowledge

We don't blame people for doing something wrong if they didn't know or couldn't know what they were doing. If you go into a room and turn on a light switch not knowing that it is wired to an explosive that will go off and kill fifty people in another room, you are not morally responsible for their deaths. Your ignorance was invincible, unavoidable. Suppose, however, that you had been warned that a mad bomber known for hooking up just this kind of device had been seen in your building and was even then being sought by building security. You would be expected not to go around turning lights on until you were assured that the switches were safe. If you did it anyway and caused an explosion, you would surely be held responsible; you couldn't claim that you didn't know this particular switch was wired, since you had good reason to suspect all switches.

In effect, we are not morally responsible for causing some event if we are unavoidably ignorant that our action will produce it. We can be held morally responsible anytime that *we should have known* about the possible consequences of what we're doing.

Freedom

The same holds true about the willingness with which we do
something. We think that if we didn't do something freely, we
shouldn't be held responsible for the consequences of what we did.
But this notion of the "freedom" with which we act, the idea of "free
will," is one of the most troublesome in philosophy. When are we
truly free in our actions?

We certainly believe that we are free; we have this sense or
consciousness that we have control over what we do; we think that in
many of our day-to-day situations we could have done something
differently from what we did; we could have acted otherwise. We
could have had the lobster instead of the steak; argued with our
relatives or bitten our tongues; taken something that didn't belong to
us or left it alone. We sometimes make a heroic effort not to do
something we think is morally wrong but are strongly tempted to do.

We believe the same is true about other people: we think that they
ordinarily are free to act or not act. We do acknowledge physical
coercion and psychological compulsions, unconscious motives and
conflicts, and where they are proven to be at work, agree that the
person acting under them was not free and, if he or she has committed
some crime under their influence, shouldn't be blamed for it. But this
begs the question of whether there are *ever* instances when we are not
being coerced beyond our will or acting under some psychological
compulsion, some external cause other than "ourselves." It presumes
that when this is not the case, we are acting freely and responsibly.

Are We Really Free? Determinism

This idea of acting freely is precisely what some philosophers have
challenged, arguing that we are never free in the sense that we are the
sole cause of whatever we do, that we make any free choice.
Determinists believe that no event ever occurs without an antecedent
cause; there are no "uncaused" events. The basis for the determinists'
contention stems largely from our scientific knowledge of the world,
e.g., from the sciences of physics and chemistry where it seems clearly
evident that all events are governed by inexorable laws of nature, that
whatever happens has to happen the way it does because of those laws.

This view of how things operate in the universe is often called *hard determinism.*

Some people might conclude that if hard determinism is true, no one can ever be held responsible for what he or she does; we are psychologically determined, our actions are unavoidable no matter how free we may feel in doing them. It appears to follow, on this view, that the murderer killed someone and the thief stole because some prior event or events (unconscious forces, perhaps, in human beings) caused them to kill and take something that belonged to someone else. Never mind that we all feel or sense or think that at least in many instances, we could have done otherwise than we did; we just aren't aware of what specific prior event occurred--e.g., in our brains--that made us act that way.

One practical consequence of this view is that education might simply be a matter of training people, by a system of rewards and punishments, to behave in socially acceptable ways. We would have to use protective measures against people whose education didn't "take," whose behavior was unacceptable to others, by locking them up or restraining them in some other way. But we couldn't be said to be "punishing" them in the retributive sense, i.e., because they knowingly and willingly did something they shouldn't have.

Indeterminism

An opposite extreme of this view is called *libertarianism,* or *indeterminism,* the idea that we are completely free in that previous causes do not force us to act, at least in many instances. Indeterminism is sometimes challenged as making no sense at all in our deterministic universe; the idea of completely "uncaused" events, in this case, acting without a prior event causing the action, is unintelligible. If it were true, it wouldn't make any more sense to blame or praise people than it does under hard determinism, because what they do apparently just "happens;" they have no control over it.

Soft Determinism

A sort of "in-between" position, called *soft determinism,* is offered by still other philosophers, e.g, Aristotle. According to this account, the causes that operate on us to act as we do are found internally in us, in our character, i.e., in our desires, purposes, and intentions. The kind of people we *are* influences what we do. Now, if we didn't give ourselves that character, how can we be responsible for the actions it prompts us to do? One answer is that our motivation to act can be influenced by reasons offered to us to change our character, and that makes us responsible for how we act.

A problem here might be to account for just what it means for us to make that change: do we make *that* decision freely, do we have control over it or not? If we do, then the whole problem of free will seems to reassert itself: just how do we do it freely? If we don't, then something outside us causes us to change and it's hard to see how we are really free and responsible. It may be that psychological conditioning (positive and negative reinforcement of our behavior, e.g.,) or reasons offered for us to change may have an effect on us, but will our subsequent behavior really then be "free" and praiseworthy? We condition animals to behave in certain ways by praising them or offering them some pleasant thing to eat when they behave as we want them to. Is that kind of conditioning all that is going on with humans as well on this "soft" account of determinism?

The Faculty of Free Will

Yet another approach to the problem of free will is to argue that we have a power, a faculty called a "will" that is moved by some "good," some object or some state of affairs it "wants," something that will satisfy it, make it content. This power must be immaterial in nature because reason and experience tell us that it cannot be compelled, determined, by an individual finite, created, object of desire; it is able to deliberate about and decide among two or more possible choices, "goods." The only object it couldn't possibly avoid choosing would be an infinite, absolute "good": God, who alone would satisfy it with total and complete contentment, "happiness."

The problem with this approach, according to a good many philosophers, is that we can't verify empirically the existence of such an immaterial power or faculty; on the contrary, we can explain the phenomenon of willing in terms of brain and other neurological processes. Its proponents counter by insisting that even though this faculty can't be identified empirically, by touching, smelling, hearing, or measuring it, our reason, reflecting on our experience of choosing, concludes that it alone can account for our consciousness that many of our acts, at least, are sufficiently under our control to call them "free."

Co-responsibility With Others

The extent of our moral responsibility often becomes particularly difficult to assess when we are cooperating in the actions of other people, especially when what we're doing together is morally suspect. If, e.g., you are a bank teller who is told by an armed robber to hand over the money in your cash drawer, you might be said to be cooperating in a robbery, but no one would accuse you of conspiracy to rob the bank. You are obviously acting under duress. Acting out of fear, under the threat of extreme violence, usually excuses us from moral responsibility. The same would hold true if you were tortured beyond reasonable endurance to do something. This kind of case is easy to understand and resolve.

It gets trickier, however, in cases where direct threat of violence is not an issue although some form of coercion (e.g., I'll lose my job or my pension) may be at work. Here some moralists make a distinction between *formal* and *material* cooperation in another person's wrongdoing.

To formally cooperate means that an agent freely (without internal or external coercion) consents to participate in somebody else's immoral action. The driver of a get-away car in a robbery can't claim that he didn't do anything wrong because he didn't enter the bank and point a weapon at anybody; he only drove the car. It's obviously clear that he consented to the robbery and his action of driving has to be considered part of the total description of what went on; he cooperated *formally* in it.

Suppose the attendant at a gas station suspects that the car she is pumping gas into may be used in a bank robbery. Is she guilty of formal cooperation with the bank robbers? The answer is most likely "no," because her action, although vital to the bank robbers, is not morally wrong in itself; it can't be considered part of the total description of the act. Nor does she intend to help them with what they are doing. Her cooperation is *material*. Material cooperation is justified when there is nothing wrong with the action a person is performing even though it's being used by someone else for his or her immoral purposes. There also has to be a good reason for cooperating: e.g., a person's job may be in jeopardy and there is no reasonable prospect of getting one as good in the immediate future.

Sometimes it becomes difficult to draw the line between formal and material cooperation. Suppose I'm a draftsperson in a plant producing nuclear weapons, and I arrive at the conscientious conviction that making these weapons is immoral. Now there's obviously nothing morally wrong, in itself, with doing drafting work; the issue is whether I may continue to do it knowing that it will be used in the design of these weapons. I no longer support making them, so would my work be formal or material cooperation if I continued at it? It's clear that if I don't do these designs, work morally indifferent in itself, my bosses will simply find someone else to do it. It looks like material cooperation in this case. If I'm a nuclear physicist, however, whose work is vital to designing and producing these weapons, if I'm that intimately connected with their final production, it's less easy to label my work as just material cooperation--especially if my particular expertise is scarce and I'm really needed to get the job done.

So, formal cooperation means that an action is done intentionally in support of some evil enterprise; it is linked inseparably with the complete description of the immoral act it is part of, and that makes the person doing it morally responsible for the act in its *entirety*.

Material cooperation means that a person's action is not morally wrong in itself, but it is being used by someone else to further his or her own evil purposes. If the person whose action is being used does not intend those purposes, he or she is not held morally responsible for the evil done but should try to get our from under the situation as soon as possible.

Chapter 4

Some Thoughts About Moral Knowledge

Can Ethical Statements Be True or False?

A major question in the study of ethics is whether statements expressing moral principles and moral judgments or other assertions about moral issues can be said to be propositions that can be true or false, i.e., can make *cognitive* claims to knowledge. How do we *know* that a particular action is right or wrong, that we ought or ought not to do it?

Scientific theories, generalizations made from empirical observation, describe the world and make predictions about what will happen there under specified physical, chemical, and biological conditions. They tell us, e.g., that given the proper conditions, hydrogen and oxygen will combine to form water; sodium and chlorine, salt. Scientific propositions are descriptive and predictive. They are tested by observation and experiment, and are said to be true or false depending on the results of those tests. Through them, we claim to know what the world is really like.

As we shall see, ethical theories and ethical judgments don't give us descriptions of how the world works; they are prescriptive, they tell us what to do or not do. Knowledge of what is right and wrong is obviously, then, not the same as scientific knowledge. The question is: what kind of knowledge is it? What kind of cognitive claims may moral theorists make?

Emotivism

Some philosophers have resolved this issue for themselves by saying that because moral statements can't be true in the same way that statements about the world are, they are simply expressions of emotion or attitude and have nothing to do with "facts." To say, e.g., "it is wrong to do x" is to say something like "I feel bad about or have a contrary attitude toward that action and so should you." No knowledge claims can be made about the content of moral statements because they have no factual meaning; they cannot be *propositions,* the only kind of statements that can be true or false.

This theory is known as *emotivism.* People who hold it are often referred to as "noncognitivists." For them, moral talk has no knowledge content; at best, it is a guide to how we should conduct ourselves or a way to influence the attitudes and feelings of others.

One root of the noncognitivist or emotivist approach is *logical positivism,* the theory that no proposition can be true unless it can in principle be verified empirically, by an appeal to "facts" out there in the world, or is true "analytically," because of its formal structure alone, not because it refers to a "fact." Mathematical propositions of the *form* "a + b = c" (2 + 2 = 4) are examples of analytically true propositions. Other examples are definitions. I can know, e.g., that the proposition: "a flying red horse is a large red quadruped equine mammal with wings" is true by definition and not because I can point to a real flying red horse. But even though I might concede that the statement "murder is unjustified homicide" is true by definition, that doesn't prove, by itself, that it is morally wrong. Nor does it make any sense for me to try to prove that it's wrong using some kind of empirical test.

All a moral statement can be, for an emotivist, is an appeal to or an expression of emotion, feeling, or attitude.

A significant problem with emotivism is how we can ever arrive at an objective view about a moral issue since there is no objective moral standard we can use to examine it. Feelings and attitudes are notoriously subjective, relative to the individual who has them. It may be true that I feel that abortion is morally wrong and you feel it is morally right, but that says nothing about the truth of the statement itself that "abortion is morally wrong (right)."

We have to conclude, on this view, that there is no way to reach objective moral judgments, that at best we can attempt to somehow persuade others, without appealing to true propositions of a moral theory, that they really should adopt our moral feelings or attitudes. The only kind of reasons we might offer them would have to be pragmatic, e.g., we might point out that certain kinds of behavior will be more conducive to a peaceful society.

There are other approaches to defining moral knowledge; I'll touch on several of them.

Naturalism

Naturalism is a theory that moral terms really stand for purely natural characteristics found in the real world.   If my watch consistently keeps time, I call it a "good" watch. All I need to know is that its parts function together properly, and I can know this from empirical observation. If naturalism is true in the world of morals, all we need to do is identify the terms for those natural characteristics that correspond to our moral terms like "good," "bad," "right," "wrong," "just," "praiseworthy," and "blameworthy"; we simply need to find the "moral facts" that exist in the world like other natural properties, and we can develop a science of morals just like we develop other empirical sciences.

The problem with naturalism is how those natural characteristics are to be seen as "moral" ones, what it is about them that makes us see *value* in them. The notion of value, after all, seems to be a critical component of all moral thinking. Consider the act of killing a human being. On its face, a description of what it involves, its "natural characteristics," the pain it may cause a person along with his or her death, seem to make it something we should avoid doing. But in spite of these "natural" features of the act, we may still see it as bringing about, in certain situations, some important value: e.g., stopping a vicious murderer's attack on ourselves or on someone else.

Another way of expressing this challenge that there is more to moral language than just expressing natural facts about the world is to make the *fact/value* distinction which means, in effect, that in moral argument, moral conclusions cannot be derived from premises that are purely factual, that have no moral language contained in them. We cannot proceed by inferential steps from purely empirical facts to moral judgments. We can't conclude, e.g., just from the physiological facts of human reproduction alone that monogamy is necessarily the best kind of family structure.

Intuitionism

Another approach to moral knowledge is *intuitionism,* which holds that some fundamental moral principles and values are self-evident to us, that we recognize them directly, "intuitively," without needing any kind of reasoning process to justify them.

The major difficulty with this theory is to explain why everybody doesn't necessarily agree on what these values and principles are, why we don't all "intuit" them in the same way. If they were so obvious, there would be no explanation for the disagreements about morality we continually run into, like whether killing or bribery or lying are always morally wrong.

Moral Reasoning

Yet another approach to knowing what is right or wrong, good or bad, is to use our reason to justify our moral beliefs. We believe, e.g., that human beings have value, worth, dignity, and that harming them, destroying their well-being in some way we can't justify is unreasonable, wrong; promoting their well-being is reasonable and right. We use reason to reach the moral principle "don't commit murder" because murder attacks an innocent victim's well-being at its very source, harms someone by depriving him or her of life.

The process becomes more difficult, of course, as situations become more complex and affect the truth of the premises used in an argument. Suppose we define murder as the direct killing of an innocent person. Is the premise that murder is morally wrong necessarily true? Would it be morally right, perhaps even obligatory, in wartime, for a government to kill innocent civilians in an enemy country if that would make its leaders give up the fight, stop the war, and save the lives of hundreds of thousands of soldiers? Would that mean that we have to change our definition of "murder" to include only situations where killing innocent persons directly *can't be justified?*

Feelings

I need to say at least a few words about feelings and emotions, and the part they may play in making moral judgments. We've seen how emotivism is challenged by pointing out that it can't produce objective judgments about moral issues since it relies wholly on subjective feelings and attitudes for its moral force. Does that mean, however, there is no role for emotions in our moral lives? We condemn a murderer who show no remorse for what he or she has done; we feel "bad" (guilt, remorse of conscience) when we have done something wrong. Conversely, we may feel "good" or satisfied about something we have done. The question, though, is just how these feelings, by themselves, are related to concrete judgments that actions are morally right or wrong.

Perhaps it's the case that specific emotions or feelings always accompany certain acts, and it could be argued that to the extent that we could establish that all human beings have these same feelings about the same acts, we would be able to identify right and wrong actions simply by the good and bad feelings that accompany them. If that were true, then it looks like emotivism would be true. It seems possible, however, to feel guilt or remorse about something we did even though we had good reasons for judging that it was the right thing to do. A soldier who kills an enemy soldier in combat may feel terrible about taking another human being's life but may have reasoned that it is still "right" to kill enemies in wartime. In effect, a feeling about an action may be separate from the judgment that it is morally right or wrong. It wouldn't do to argue in rebuttal that it's just a case of matching the right feeling to the appropriate kind of action; to argue that way would be to introduce some outside criterion to make the correct match, and that would undercut the whole point of emotivism.

Feelings of Care and Concern for Others

Some philosophers believe that care and concern for others may be more important than appeals to rational, universal moral principles such as: "in any given situation do whatever will do the most good for the most people." On this view, my sympathy for a person suffering severe pain might be the criterion by which I would agree that he or she should be free to stop that pain by committing suicide and that it would be perfectly all right for me to help him or her do it.   The question, however, arises as to whether feelings of care, concern, and sympathy toward others in a given situation are, by themselves, enough to make a particular situation right, or whether it is important to determine how care, concern, and sympathy should be directed. If my child is drowning along with a scientist who is on the verge of discovering a cure for AIDS and I can save only one of them, are my love and concern for my child enough to make my decision to save her right, or must my care, concern, and sympathy be for the many thousands of people whose lives might be saved by this scientist?   If the latter, some additional criterion beyond my feelings of care and concern has to be introduced in order to make my judgment correct. The intensity of the feeling doesn't seem to serve that purpose; it's highly probable that my feelings will surely be more intense in the case of my child than they will be for people whom I may not even know.

Chapter 5

Cultural Moral Relativism

Only Society's Rules Count

As I noted in earlier chapters, moral relativists hold that there is no objective standard, no norm, we can all refer to to insure that our moral judgments are correct and that they apply at any time to all of us whenever we are situated in identical circumstances. One version of this approach to morality is *cultural relativism,* the idea that the practices or customs or *mores* of the particular society we live in are the measure of what's morally right or wrong.

Cultural anthropologists tell us that there are significant moral differences among communities and societies, that actions which some groups of people think are perfectly acceptable, morally speaking, might be abhorrent to others. Some examples: abandoning aged members of a society so that they will no longer be a drain on its resources; killing female babies in societies where male babies are preferred; genital mutilation of females; polygamy, and the practice of slavery. Some ancient cultures thought it proper to eat their dead; others believed (like us) that the dead should be buried.

It's easy to make moral judgments if cultural relativism is true because those actions a society approves of are morally permissible and those it disapproves of are morally unacceptable. Note that no reasoning process is involved here: just do or avoid whatever your culture tells you to do or avoid.

Some people find that this strategy nicely accommodates their own line of thinking: business people, e.g., often believe that it's permissible to bribe a country's government officials in order to win a contract because "that's the way *they* do things."

Challenges to Cultural Moral Relativism

Some of the objections to cultural relativism as a satisfactory account of morality seem obvious. How, e.g., would we ever argue that one social group's practices are better or worse than another's without some objective moral guideline, one that is independent of any group's or individual's beliefs, to compare them with? For the same reason, there would never be any grounds for one society to urge another to "better" or reform its practices. It doesn't seem to make much sense, e.g., for the United Nations to propose a universal declaration of human rights when any "rights" a member of a community has are specified by that community's practices which may differ significantly from what other social groups' (including whole countries) are.

A more subtle challenge to cultural relativism is to point out that its proponents who argue from the *fact* of diverse cultural beliefs in the world to the conclusion that no objective moral standard can exist make a logical mistake. Such a conclusion just doesn't follow from the argument's premises; it attempts to derive what *is* the case from premises that represent *beliefs.* What is real doesn't follow necessarily from what is believed. Another way looking at this fallacy is to point out that just because nurses may differ in how they administer IV's, it doesn't follow that no standard nursing practice for that procedure exists; or that from the fact that children play sandlot football by different rules there are no standard rules for the game.

There is one more objection to cultural relativism. It's easy to say "when in Rome, do as the Romans," but it's often hard to decide where "Rome's" boundaries begin and end. In the United States, e.g., there are people who believe in practicing polygamy; others refuse, on religious grounds, to authorize blood transfusions for their children. Both practices are overruled by US law which may simple reflect the cultural or religious preferences of the majority. Is US law unfair to all these people? If effect, if cultural relativism is true, whose cultural practices, beliefs, or preferences made into rules should take precedence in a pluralist society/ Does the majority have the right to enforce its rules on the minority culture? On what grounds, except by saying "that's simply the way most of us do it here (wherever 'here' means)"?

Some philosophers suggest that in spite of the surface differences in the moral practices of societies, there are really common standards, shared values operating at a deeply underlying level in all of them. Strict cultural relativism, however, would not recognize these values explicitly since only the particular practices, not their foundation, are what count.

An example of such a value would be the need to preserve a society and insure its continuation. This may account for surface practices like infanticide, polygamy, forced female circumcision, and neglect of older members in a society. In some tribes, killing female infants would keep the number of males and females in their society proportionate and would avoid a shortage of males who do the hunting. If infant mortality were chronically high and there were more females than males in the tribe, polygamy would guarantee sufficient new offspring. Female genital mutilation would be seen as a way to insure marital fidelity on the part of women and preserve the integrity of families. If there were shortages of food, banishing the elderly from the tribe would make certain that there was enough food for the young who are its future.

This same value, preservation and continuation of a society, may underlie practices in other cultures that are totally at odds with these. Since, however, the core of cultural relativism is that only the practices themselves count, that members of a society are simply expected to do what their ancestors have done from time immemorial, there doesn't seem to be any point in a direct appeal to this value to justify either society's practices.

MORAL THEORY: A MORE SOPHISTICATED APPROACH

As I see it, cultural moral relativism has too many weaknesses to serve as a sound way of making moral judgments. I'll proceed now to investigate some examples of more sophisticated approaches to analyzing and understanding morality: moral theories. Let's begin with *utilitarianism*.

Chapter 6

Utilitarianism

Jeremy Bentham: Pleasure and Pain

Utilitarianism is probably the best example of a fully consequentialist moral theory (one which holds that only the consequences of an action, its results, the state of affairs it produces, the preferences it satisfies count in making moral judgments). A modern proponent of this approach to a moral theory was Jeremy Bentham (1748-1832) who believed that there are two fundamental masters which govern our actions: pleasure and pain. Bentham thought that the criterion for judging whether actions are morally right or wrong lies in their *utility*, their tendency to contribute to the happiness of an individual or to a body of individuals making up a community by adding to their pleasure or diminishing their pain. Governments, in particular, are especially concerned with the happiness of the community--whose happiness, for Bentham, amounts to the sum total of the interests of the individuals comprising it.

To make a correct moral judgment, Bentham argued, one has to consider how much pleasure and pain a particular action will produce as measured by their intensity, duration, certainty or uncertainty (how sure is it that they will in fact be produced by the action), nearness or remoteness (how soon they will follow upon completing the action), fecundity (how much pleasure and pain will continue to be caused by that kind of action in the future), purity (e.g., to what extent the pleasure generated is untainted by pain), and extent (how many people are affected). He thought this procedure which involved giving a plus value to the pleasure and a minus value to the pain made it possible to *quantify* the total amount of pleasure and pain associated with any particular action.

By following this process (known as Bentham's "hedonic calculus"), all that is needed to make a moral judgment is to simply add the values assigned algebraically: a net plus result means that the action is morally right and a negative result makes it immoral.

For Bentham, then, an action is morally right when it conforms to the principle of utility: bringing about the most pleasure, happiness, as he put it, for an individual or, as appropriate, the most people. An action that doesn't conform to it is morally wrong. He held that this principle can't be proven since everything else in morality depends on it; it is the *first principle* of morality.

Measuring Pleasure and Pain

Bentham believed that pleasure is synonymous with words like "benefit," "good," "profit," "advantage," and "happiness," while "mischief," "evil," and "unhappiness" meant the same as "pain." Further, he thought that one pleasure is as good as another as long as they are measured along the same scale. He is reported to have said that as long as the quantity of pleasure at stake is the same, pushpin (a children's game played with stick pins) is as good as poetry.

An obvious problem for the hedonic calculus is how to go about giving pleasure and pain an exact quantitative value so that it can be applied correctly. How are we to measure the amount of elation or discomfort we are experiencing in a particular situation? In addition, since we're supposed to care about the pleasure and pain of everyone affected by an action or of all the members of a community if the community's interests are at stake, how can we be sure that we will give everyone his or her due, how do we calculate the magnitude of their elation or discomfort?

Bentham recognized that it was difficult to supply a precise unit of measurement for this process but believed that we are nevertheless able to give a reasonable although not mathematically precise weight to the amount of pleasure and pain associated with any action: sufficient, at least for the purpose of giving it a moral evaluation.

John Stuart Mill

John Stuart Mill (1806-1873), a friend and disciple of Bentham, agreed with Bentham's fundamental approach to making moral judgments. Like Bentham, he believed that right and wrong should be decided by asking whether an action tends to produce happiness or unhappiness. Since he uses the words "tends to," it's apparent that he understands that we can only estimate what effects an action will have based on our own or others' previous experience with that kind of action.

Mill also agreed with Bentham that it's not just the agent's happiness that counts but the happiness of others affected by his or her action. He was concerned with producing happiness on the whole, in the aggregate; the more happiness an action produces, the more valuable it is.

A common phrase used by some contemporary utilitarians to express Mill's idea is *producing the most good consequences* (results, states of affairs, satisfaction of interests) *for the most people* (or, sentient beings for those who wish to include at least higher-order animals in the calculation. I say "higher-order" to suggest that even for these people there may be a limit as to which non-human beings should be included: e.g., cockroaches?)

Mill's fundamental criterion, then, for judging the morality of actions was happiness, as it was for Bentham, but he disagreed with Bentham's claim that the *quantity* of pleasure and pain an action tended to generate was what counted in making moral judgments. Mill insisted on distinguishing *quality* among pleasures, e.g., he believed that the pleasures of the mind are surely on a higher level than mere sensual pleasure. To paraphrase him, it's better to be a human being dissatisfied than a pig satisfied. In effect, he would not likely agree with Bentham that pushpin could ever be as good as poetry.

Some Thoughts About Pleasure and Pain

It's not too hard to understand what "pain" means; practically anything that causes us discomfort falls under that concept. We ordinarily want to avoid any pain whatsoever. We may tolerate pain as an unavoidable accompaniment of a means to a good end, like the pain of the dentist's drill or the pain that goes with physical conditioning. It's difficult, then, to fault Bentham's equating pain with "mischief," "evil," and "unhappiness."

Is it as easy to equate pleasure with happiness? Mill thought so. He claimed that it was a mistake to think that the idea of "utility" in his and Bentham's theories meant something more high-minded than pleasure.

Now it seems clear that for both Bentham and Mill, the happiness they had in mind was certainly not just sensual pleasure which we usually think of as having to do with tactile experiences like eating, drinking and sex. One can always ask whether a particular sensual pleasure is really good, or beneficial; whether it will really make a person "happy." Surely sensual pleasures are not the simple equivalent of pursuing and achieving knowledge, the satisfaction of knowing more about ourselves and our world. While we shouldn't rule out sensual pleasure entirely from the meaning of happiness, it just doesn't make sense to think that that's all it means. So, what are we really talking about?

Many of us have experienced the good feeling, the joy, the sense of achievement that accompanies solving a difficult problem in math or logic or comprehending some writer's complex exposition of a subject, or the enjoyment we get from the fine arts, the stimulation of intellectual conversation, playing or watching sports, or making some special contribution to one of the many communities we belong to. There is even satisfaction in making sacrifices for the good of others: our families, e.g., or friends or country.

We feel exhilaration at playing a sport well. What is that exhilaration, anyway? It can't just be a sensual feeling; it's absurd to believe, e.g., that the members of a football team that has just won a grueling physical battle with a tough opponent find any joy, benefit, advantage, satisfaction, happiness in their sore muscles and joints. It's obviously their sense of accomplishment that overrides their physical pain and elates them.

Aristotle said that all our activity seeks some good, some end, some achievement, and the overall good we are after is happiness. We are goal-oriented creatures; we constantly strive to accomplish good things in our lives, to realize our life plans, and we find a sense of good feeling and contentment--both in the activity and in our accomplishments. Happiness, for Aristotle, is found precisely in rational activity (rational because it has to do with ordering means to ends, achieving things, and because human beings are concerned with contemplating truths that are unchangeable) over a lifetime, hand-in-hand with virtuous conduct.

Achievement isn't always easy, obviously; we may sometimes experience real pain or suffering on the way to reaching many of our goals, but the satisfaction, the contentment, we realize when we get there usually eases the memory of the hardships we ran into along the way. Many times we're willing to boast about the obstacles we had to overcome as a true measure of what we've accomplished.

An interesting question is whether achieving the goal grants us contentment, or whether what we're really after is the contentment itself, the pleasure, the "good feeling" that accompanies successful activity. It seems, if we reflect on it, that very often, when we deliberately set out to realize pleasure or contentment or joy, they elude us, vanish, whereas when the goal-seeking activity preoccupies us, the contentment, the pleasure seems to flow along with it and we hear ourselves saying, "this is really fun."

These musings on pleasure and happiness serve to suggest that it is not unreasonable to equate happiness with pleasure (taken in its widest sense, not just understood as "sensuality"). "Happiness" seems readily synonymous with words like "contentment," "joy," "satisfaction," "elation." The question for utilitarians is how we measure happiness when we're trying to use it as the criterion for making moral decisions.

Is it really possible to "quantify" contentment, joy, satisfaction, or elation as Bentham thought? His approach to measuring quantity of pleasure reduces to the psychological feeling, sensibility, as he put it, associated with an action; how do we measure that? Is it "depth" of feeling? What common unit do we use in that case? Isn't it possible that one person may feel more deeply about what is going on in the case of a particular action than others? Is this person's depth of feeling offset by simply adding up the feelings of the other people involved so that even if they feel less deeply, their feelings, taken together, count more in the final decision on whether to perform an action or not?

To illustrate this point, take a somewhat oversimplified example of a group of people waiting in line on a cold winter morning to board a bus. Suppose an older man among them is obviously suffering from the cold more than the others are; should the first person in line give up his or her place to that man? Most of us would likely say "yes" out of simple compassion for another human being. The issue, however, is whether utilitarian moral theory would *oblige* the person at the head of the line to give up his or her place on the grounds that the older man is feeling more pain than he or she is. Further, would each of the persons ahead of this man have to make that same moral judgment on those same grounds relative to his or her own place in the line?

Consider the two factors in Bentham's hedonic calculus that seem to me to be the most relevant in this situation: the intensity of the pleasure or pain felt and the number of people who will be affected by moving or not moving this person to the head of the line. It might be apparent that he is suffering the cold more than any other individual and that would be enough to oblige each of them to move him ahead. But is that really what Bentham's calculus demands? Because the number of people affected also enters into the tally, does intensity of feeling give way to the numbers, i.e., should the simple fact that there are more people ahead of him in line who are also suffering some degree of pain count against giving him any special consideration?

On Bentham's account, requiring that the sum of the pleasure or pain of all the individuals affected by an action has to be the final measure of the overall pleasure or pain associated with it, so it looks like the intensity of the pain suffered by the elderly man has to be compared with the aggregate of the intensity of pain being suffered by all the others, even though their *individual* pain might not be as intense as his.

Does Mill's qualitative approach to measuring pleasure work any better than Bentham's insistence on quantity? How, especially, do we sort out whose happiness should be preferred, qualitatively speaking, when we're dealing with several people who will be affected by an action?

Mill's answer to distinguishing among pleasures on the basis of quality was that we simply need to ask experienced people which of two pleasures they prefer. Their preference will be affected by the "higher faculties": their intellect, feeling and imagination, and moral sentiment will certainly distinguish really valuable pleasures from mere sensual ones, at least. No one would want to be reduced to the level of desiring the pleasures of a beast. It's clear that people recognize that some pleasures are intrinsically more valuable than others.

But Mill's answer still leaves some practical puzzles. Just how do these higher faculties operate to dictate preferences? It's doubtful, e.g., that reason alone can account for what gives or should give people satisfaction; not everybody prefers opera over hockey games--even though a rational account might be available to explain the superior value of the first over the second. Some people will still prefer hockey. As for feelings and imagination as guidelines for value, they are notoriously subjective. It's evident, I think, from our everyday experience, that many people are "happier" watching or participating in a sport than in listening to any opera whatsoever. One could argue, I suppose, that they ought to know better; Mill thought that even though some people knew that certain pleasures were more valuable than, say, sensual ones, they often pursued the less valuable anyway because they had allowed their intellectual discrimination to grow dull. It's also possible that some people are less generously endowed with these higher faculties than others. But if feelings and imagination are among the higher faculties and might lead some people less richly endowed with them to prefer less intellectual pleasure, it's hard to quarrel with that preference--on Mill's own account.

The idea of a "moral sentiment" among the higher faculties at least raises the question of just what that might be. Mill doesn't tell us what he means by it. Is it some kind of intuition that is objectively the same for everybody? If it is, why isn't it sufficient by itself to tell us whether an action is right or wrong? Why would we need the utilitarian calculus? If it isn't a direct intuition telling us what's right or wrong about an action, but has the character of a feeling that may well be subjective, relative to each individual, it's hard to see how it could serve as an objective criterion for deciding the intrinsic value of one particular pleasure over another.

Mill is right, of course, in claiming that we do have to discriminate among pleasure or consequences as situations demand; we need to decide which pleasure, result, outcome is more valuable than another. We may be obliged, e.g., to help a seriously ill person even though that may get in the way of our doing something more pleasant for ourselves. Our job may require us to be somewhere or do something when we would prefer to be in some other place doing something else. Feelings may play a part here: suppose, e.g., that the person needing help is a good friend or relative. In other circumstances, we may have to do what reason dictates is the better course.

The question is whether, in every case, the higher quality pleasure *has* to be preferred. Are we always obliged to choose intellectual activities over those that may simply be entertaining?

Weighing Consequences

The issue here may perhaps become clearer if we use the terminology often employed by contemporary utilitarians as the meaning of happiness associated with an action: the "consequences" it will produce. It might appear that it's easier to deal with effects, results, or outcomes because they can be expressed in more concrete terms than "happiness" or "pleasure." But even so the process is often perplexing.

Consider the difficulty in comparing good and bad consequences in terms of "dollars" (monetary costs and benefits) and human lives. Can they be compared equally on the scale of utility?

Suppose a company finds out before marketing a particular product that a flaw in its design poses a highly probable threat of serious harm or even death to some of the people who are going to use it. Should that fact be enough to force the company to redesign the item or decide not to put it on the market? Or should its decision be based on comparing the cost of redesigning the product with an estimate of the damages the company may have to pay for any harm done to people who will buy and use it?

Making that comparison isn't all that complex. First, establish, from life insurance statistical tables, what a person's projected earnings are over a lifetime, adjust it for loss of earnings for whether people are just harmed or killed, and multiply those figures as appropriate by the estimated number of victims. Finally, calculate what redesigning the product will cost. If that cost outweighs the cost of compensating victims, i.e., if the cost-benefit ratio isn't favorable, it looks like the right economic decision is to scrap the redesign and go ahead with manufacturing and marketing the item. But is it the correct utilitarian decision? It could be argued, I suppose, that the company's dollar values represent the value of its earning to people: managers, employees, shareholders, and the members of the communities supported by the company; maybe that's what the utilitarian calculus would have to consider in this situation.

The Ford Motor Company is alleged to have used this kind of reasoning in the seventies when it decided to market the *Pinto* knowing that there was a high probability that the gas tank would catch fire in rear-end collisions occurring at certain speeds. Would a utilitarian think that the Company's decision was morally correct? Is the value of even one human life really commensurate with any amount of money for purposes of utilitarian calculation?

Some utilitarians like to define the consequences that are at issue in moral decision-making in terms of the individual interests and preferences of the people included in the situation that calls for a moral judgment. But here, again, how do we get an objective "fix" (one independent of what a group or any individual may think) on the *quality* of one person's preferences or interests compared with another's? If quality can't be compared, then it seems like we're forced into a simple aggregation of some people's interests over others--in effect, only the numbers count. That was the puzzle we wrestled with in the chapter on judging the moral character of an action when we tried to determine, in the case of the mad bomber, whether the lives of the people in one group could be considered more valuable than the lives of those in another.

Are some lives more valuable, on utilitarian grounds, so numbers wouldn't necessarily be the correct way to calculate utility? Suppose I could divert a runaway train on one of two tracks. On one track are ten workers who will be killed if I send the train there; there are only two workers on the other track. The utilitarian answer seems clear here: save the ten workers. But, what if the two people on the other track aren't workers but medical researchers (never mind, for the moment, how they got there) on the verge of discovering a vaccine or a cure for AIDS; aren't their lives more valuable not to themselves, necessarily, but to thousands of people who would prefer to be cured of that dreaded disease? Looking at the situation from this perspective, we would have to add up the preferences of more people than just those involved in the immediate situation.

The issue of quality of preference does seem straightforward enough in certain situations: e.g., when we're driving along in traffic and hear an ambulance's siren, most of us in the line of traffic think it appropriate to move over and let the ambulance by.   Saving one person's life seems preferable to the desire the rest of us have to get to our respective destinations on time.   But there are other situations where it's not so clear.

Suppose the state wants to put a highway through a family's property that has great sentimental value for its members because many generations of its forebears have lived there.   Is this family's preference to preserve the old homestead more important than the aggregate preferences of many more people to have an efficient (and perhaps safer) route for their travels?

What if the state wants to establish group homes for the mentally disadvantaged throughout selected residential neighborhoods as part of the patients' treatment and rehabilitation? May the property owners in those neighborhoods claim that their preferences for keeping up the value of their residences is more important than the treatment of the people the state is trying to assist by normalizing, as far as possible, their living conditions?

If a business executive is trying to decide whether to pay a bribe to get a lucrative contract, is it enough to consider just his or her shareholders, employees, and the communities that depend on his or her company? Why would their interests be more important than those of the shareholders, employees and communities of the competitors against whom the executive is bidding--unless in terms of sheer numbers?

In the end, the utilitarian calculus seems to eliminate, except in some clearly defined situations (like getting out of the way of an ambulance when someone's life is at stake) any possibility of comparing, on any kind of solidly objective basis, the quality of individual preferences. The calculus reduces, for the most part, to adding up the preferences of individuals affected by an action and letting the preferences of the many outweigh the preferences of the few.

Other Challenges to Utilitarianism

There are some other problems generated by utilitarian moral theory.

It does not regard any action as morally wrong in itself, i.e., just because of the *kind* of action it is. Murder, suicide, genocide, rape, torture, slavery, theft, and deceit have a morally reproachful characteristic woven into their very definitions and, for many moralists, are never justified. The utilitarian, however, will never say that an action is morally wrong until all its relevant, reasonably foreseeable consequences are examined and their respective utility calculated. It follows that in certain situations, it may be necessary to act in ways that may seem, on their face, morally repugnant, e.g., to deliberately and directly kill innocent people if that would save a significant number of other lives. This was likely President Harry Truman's belief in 1945 when he ordered atomic bombs dropped on Hiroshima and Nagasaki, Japan: the deaths of 140,000 noncombatants that would force the Japanese leadership to surrender and stop the war seemed to be outweighed by the greater number of casualties and deaths that his advisors predicted would result from a direct invasion of the Japanese islands. It's conceivable, of course, that he did not think these people were innocent since they probably supported their leaders in the war and were, in some cases, ready to fight any invading Allied forces. Whether his action was just a case of killing innocent civilians or not is still controversial for many people. But even if they were innocent noncombatants, it looks like utilitarian moral theory would justify killing them.

In effect, for utilitarians, a good end could justify the means to it, regardless of how heinous those means might be in themselves.

Another difficulty for utilitarians is determining just who is affected by an action, its "reach," so to speak. Is it all right, e.g., for someone to enjoy an expensive meal at a restaurant when the price of that meal might feed a starving family in Somalia for a month? Would all of us have to donate our surplus wealth, that amount over and above what is immediately needed for ourselves and our families, until there were no longer any starving people anywhere in the world? If everybody did that, what would happen to our own economies? After a time, if none of us bought any of the commodities produced over and above our immediate living needs, where would the surplus wealth needed to provide for the rest of the world come from? I exaggerate, surely; the utilitarian might well point out that all of us don't have to give up *every bit* of our surplus; just enough of it to satisfy the utilitarian measure required here.

If my child and a scientist who is on the verge of finding a cure for cancer that may save thousands of lives are both drowning, and I can only save one of them, who must I save?

In effect, how do we determine that we're doing the most good "on the whole?" Must we consider the entire world as "the whole" every time we make a moral judgment?

Justice

The concept of justice poses yet another problem for utilitarian moral theory which seems to require that it would be morally right, e.g., to punish innocent people if that would clearly prevent others from doing some serious harm to other people or a community. In a famous case in Guilford, England, some years ago, authorities tried, convicted, and sentenced several people to long terms in prison for planting a bomb that killed a number of patrons in a local pub. The prosecution allegedly knew those convicted were actually innocent, but because they were suspected of having links to the Irish Republican Army (IRA), believed that making a case against them and punishing them would help deter future IRA terrorist bombings. The convictions were overturned fifteen years later when the prosecution's apparent deception became public.

If this account is correct, an injustice was clearly done to these people, but it seems, on utilitarian grounds, that if the deception had not been discovered and further IRA bombings had in fact been deterred, the punishment of these people might have been morally justified.

Perhaps the best answer utilitarians could give to this weakness in the theory is that injustice will most likely not produce greater good, in the long run, at least, and should always be avoided. But there is still the nagging suspicion that a case might be made in some given situation, and "always" might be too restrictive a condition.

Act and Rule Utilitarianism

Some utilitarians, acknowledging these challenges to the theory, have suggested that a distinction between *act* and *rule* utilitarianism will take care of them. On this account, the good consequences produced by observing a *general rule* to refrain from a certain kind of action may well outweigh the good that a specific action of this kind would produce on its own in a concrete situation. More overall utility will likely result, e.g., if everyone observes the rule to never directly take the life of an innocent person ("murder) or never commit grave injustice even though doing so, in some particular instance, would generate more good than evil consequences.

Act utilitarians claim that this distinction attacks the very foundation of utilitarianism which, as they see it, requires that we must always select that individual action among possible alternatives that will produce overall good consequences for the most people in a particular situation.

Consequences Are Important but Maybe They're Not All That Counts

These objections to utilitarianism do not destroy the importance of the consequences an action generates, the state of affairs it will produce, for making a moral judgment about it. We can't describe or understand an act without considering what will *happen* if someone does it. We do sometimes need to weigh the "greater good of the many" over the good of the "few." The difficulty lies in the idea that consequences are all that count in the sense that an action cannot be called morally right or wrong until all its foreseeable consequences and *only* those consequences are considered. Another approach to making moral judgments takes into account an action's consequences, but may decide that it is morally wrong before the person doing it considers *everything* it will cause; the immediate consequences that are always associated with it may prove to be so evil that any further good results it may bring about can never make it morally right. There may be certain rights, e.g., that individuals have like the right to life or to bodily and psychological integrity that can't be overridden by the greater good of the many; it may be that the preferences or interests of the majority do not always outweigh, in the aggregate, the preferences or interests of the minority. We'll explore an example of this model of a moral theory next: *natural law.*

Chapter 7

Natural Law

St. Thomas Aquinas' Version

Utilitarianism, as we have seen, is a moral theory that relies on an action's good and evil consequences, the state of affairs, the results, it produces as the ultimate criterion for determining whether it is morally right or wrong. We'll now look at natural law, a theory which acknowledges that is necessary but not sufficient to consider consequences in making moral judgments.

This theory has a long history and comes in several versions. All of them look to human nature in some way as the foundation of morality. The version I propose to briefly describe here is based in large part on the thinking of St. Thomas Aquinas (c. 1224-1274) who, in turn, owed a lot of what he thought about morality to Aristotle and some other philosophical predecessors. Much of Aquinas' thinking serves as the philosophical support for Catholic moral theology, so familiarity with this theory may provide a better understanding of some of the current controversies associated with Catholic teaching in such areas as abortion, artificial contraception, the use of condoms to promote safe sex, euthanasia, and homosexuality.

I should note here that while many ethicists follow this natural-law tradition, they do not necessarily agree with all the conclusions of the arguments I propose to discuss in what follows. Much of what I will describe here will reflect the *stronger* interpretation of the theory exemplified, e.g., by the official moral teaching of the Catholic Church.

The Definition of Natural Law

For Aquinas, natural law is a product of *practical reason,* reason oriented to action, developing precepts, principles, rules for how we are to act to be happy. He defined natural law as the participation of human reason in the eternal law of God. I'll try to explain concisely what he means by all this, concentrating on my understanding of the *philosophical* ideas that lie behind this theory.

Natural Human Inclinations, Primary and Secondary Precepts of the Natural Law

Aquinas observed that we have certain fundamental *inclinations* we are prompted to satisfy: e.g., preserving our lives; having and educating children; seeking knowledge and understanding of ourselves and the universe we live in, and living in society with others. There are "goods" (values) that correspond to those inclinations. As soon as we encounter them in our life experience, we know immediately that they are valuable to us, that they serve our well-being. *Practical* reason forms, on the basis of this immediate knowledge, the very first, primary, precept of natural law: "do good and avoid evil."

It's important to stress that this precept, or principle, is not innate, handed to us, as it were, with all our other native human capacities; practical reason *generates* it.

As we comprehend the goods (values) fundamental to our well-being, we also understand that we "ought" to pursue them, and that ought is expressed in other primary precepts formed by practical reason: e.g., "preserve your life"; "carry on the human species"; "live in mutually supportive communities with others."

At this level, these precepts are all known without any discursive, inferential proofs one from the other; forming them depends on our coming into contact with and recognizing values fundamental to our well-being.

Secondary Precepts

Practical reason functions, then, as a lawgiver; it lays down for us the requirement to pursue what is good for us and shun what is bad for beings with a nature like ours. Its primary precepts are stated at a very general level. More specific, "secondary" rules for just what is good and bad for a person and must be done or avoided are developed out of each person's life experience. A secondary rule of action might be derived from a primary one, e.g., the rule that "the lives of innocent persons are not to be taken directly" is based on the general requirement not to harm others.

Life's Contingencies Sometimes Make It Hard to Classify Actions

It's not hard to grasp practical reason's rules of action at the very general level, but applying more specific rules to individual cases, deciding what moral species a particular action belongs to, is often difficult because of the various contingencies associated with actions. If, e.g., I take this person's property against his or her will when it's the only way to save another person's life, am I stealing or performing an act of mercy? Is removing a nasogastric feeding tube from a dying patient a case of starving that person or is it just stopping a medical procedure that is no longer effective?

Natural Law Doesn't Mean Deriving "Ought from Is"

It's important to note that St. Thomas did not mean that we derive what we should or should not do directly from the *facts* we know about the kind of being we are but from "within," as it were, from our own inclinations, from our comprehension of what "good" means, what is "valuable" to us, and from our experience with life's situations. His theory does not demand that we determine "ought" directly from "is."

Natural Law is a Participation in the Eternal Law

As I understand him, Aquinas saw natural law, human practical reason determining what we ought to do or not do, as participating in

God's direction and governance of the whole world--the *eternal law*. God has given human beings practical reason so that we can come to know, *on our own,* what God the Creator wants for us, how He wants us to *freely* act in our own interest, to do what is good for beings with our kind of nature, *to be happy.* In effect, when we obey our own right reason, we obey God.

The Relationship of Natural Law to Positive Laws of the State

Some of the *positive* laws enacted by states that provide penalties for their violation overlap with and may even be deduced directly from natural law (murder, theft, and perjury, e.g., are forbidden by both). Others can't be deduced directly from natural law precepts--e.g., traffic laws or laws establishing specific titles to property-but they are subject to natural law's oversight. Positive laws can violate natural law (e.g., positive laws that forbid marriage between different races) and, therefore, can have no binding force--morally speaking. Since positive laws are designed to promote human welfare, the natural-law moralist can argue that the source of their obligation stems, ultimately, from the obligation natural law imposes because the root of that obligation is precisely overall human well-being.

The Moral Integrity of an Act

So far, I've outlined a very general description of what natural law is all about. Now I'll attempt a more specific account of its approach to making moral decisions.

According to the natural-law moralist, every action we do must have moral integrity, i.e., it must be:

o morally good *in itself;*

o good in its *circumstances,* the situation in which it is done;

o done with a morally good *motive.*

If any one of these elements is not satisfied, the entire action is morally wrong. Let's examine each of them to see just what the natural-law moralist has in mind here.

Intrinsically Wrong Actions

Reason finds certain actions so evidently contrary to those goods, values, that correspond to our natural inclinations that they are always morally wrong. The rules forbidding them do not allow exceptions-no matter how many good consequences they might produce overall. Some examples:

o murder;

o suicide;

o direct killing for reasons of mercy (euthanasia);

o adultery;

o rape;

o theft;

o deceit;

o slavery.

The key to understanding what makes these actions intrinsically wrong is the idea that every action must first be examined in its *object* to determine what makes it the *kind* of act it is, what it is that is being done, what end the agent intends, plans, to accomplish with it." (It's important to note that the "object" of an act is distinct from the motive with which it done, *why* the agent is doing it. More on this later.)

There are actions that can be described as morally "neutral" relative to their objects. The object of walking, e.g., is to move from one place to another; talking, to convey information, feelings, opinions; lifting, to raise something from one position to another; using a tool, to shape something. For purposes of making moral judgments, however, these descriptions of objects are incomplete, abstract; we have to ask what these acts are ultimately intended to bring about, what their consequences considered along with their concrete circumstances are intended to accomplish, in order to fully describe the kind of acts they are, *morally* speaking. Let me explain what I mean here.

Consequences and Circumstances

The consequences of an action, its effects, the state of affairs it brings about are, of course, important in deciding what kind of act it is but they're not always the final criterion. It should be obvious that not every action that causes harm to someone in the physical order is automatically wrong. A surgeon who cuts off a person's gangrenous toes is certainly causing a kind of harm to the patient by destroying his or her body's physical integrity but that doesn't mean the surgeon is violating the moral law.   Producing that particular harm in the physical order also brings about a good effect: saving the patient's life. Killing a person is obviously harmful, but there may be a legitimate reason for taking his or her life. So, we need to first determine, in the cases where harmful consequences are involved, whether the harm an action causes someone is *justified* or not.

It is possible that consequences can, on their own, make an action immoral: suppose, for instance, that it produces *only* evil consequences or it always produces more evil than good. Ordinarily, though, we have to look first at the circumstances surrounding the action along with its consequences to finally decide what kind of act it is.

It often turns out that the description of an act has a feature built into it that makes it *essentially* morally wrong and, as a result, always forbidden. The physical act of talking, e.g., can be an act of telling the truth or withholding the truth from someone who as a right to it--in which case we call it a *lie*. Lifting up a gold watch from a jeweler's counter can either be indicating that it's what a buyer wants and that he or she is ready to pay for it, or it's taking it without paying--and then we call it *theft*. Drilling into someone's safe because he or she asked you to is different from drilling into it without the owner's permission.

Note that in the kind of actions we've just been talking about, both the harm done to someone and the circumstances in which it is done taken together may make the action intrinsically wrong. What's going on here is that we collapse some of the circumstances surrounding an action into its *full moral description*. When an action is completely described by including its consequences and any circumstances that are *always* part of its description, that are built into the very essence of what the action is, it often receives its final moral character right then and there. In effect, these actions have morality built into their very definition. Their object, then, what the person doing them intends, his or her proximate end, includes consequences and circumstances. He or she intends to tell a lie, not just say something to somebody; to steal a watch, not just lift it off the counter.

Consider the act of murder. It's not that the natural-law ethicist can never justify taking a human life; he or she will concede that there may be situations when it is morally acceptable to kill someone: e.g., an enemy soldier fighting in a war where his or her side is an unjust aggressor, or defending against someone who is threatening a person's life or even, in some cases, his or her property--as long as the death that results is proportionate to the good that the act of killing produces. In these situations, the full object of the act giving it its moral species is more than just homicide: it's "self-defense."

It does seem curious that killing another human being can be initially described as morally neutral in its object--like walking, talking, lifting, or using a tool, that it doesn't become morally wrong until the circumstances in which it is done are collapsed into its description. After all, killing someone is the most direct violation of that fundamental inclination we all have to stay alive; it obviously destroys forever the possibility of any happiness for the person who is killed. That, however, is how the natural-law moralist sees it. What makes an act of killing always morally wrong, what makes it *murder,* comes from two key elements found in the circumstances, the situation in which it is done: the victim's *innocence* and the fact that his or her life is taken *directly.* (I'll talk about the moral justification for *indirectly* killing an innocent person later, when I take up the principle of "double-effect.")

One question the natural-law moralist has to answer is why, if we can collapse the circumstances into an action's essential description and decide it is always wrong, the reverse shouldn't be true: can't an action be judged morally right by the same process? Take abortion, as an example. If a mother's life or health is at stake, or she was raped, or believes that one more mouth to feed is too much for her financially overburdened family to handle, why can't these situations, these circumstances, become an essential element of the act?

One answer is that when there are circumstances and/or consequences that always, necessarily, accompany a particular action and are sufficient to specify it as always, *intrinsically,* wrong, additional circumstances or good consequences can never override them, nullify their contribution to what an act *already is.* Once the act is definitively characterized as morally wrong, there is no way to make it something else by adding another set of circumstances or consequences to it. In the case of abortion, e.g., arguing from the premise that it is an act of directly taking an innocent life, there is no way to alter its essential definition as murder.

More on Circumstances

By now the importance of the circumstances surrounding an action should be evident. We may start with a neutral, abstract description of an action, but we also need to look at the situation in which it is performed to decide what kind of action it is. We've seen how an action is specified as lying, theft, or murder only when key circumstances in which the action occurs are taken into account.

Other examples where circumstances are decisive for specifying an action as intrinsically wrong would be sexual relations with someone other than one's spouse (adultery, extra-marital sex) or price gouging in selling merchandise.

Circumstances involving "who," "when," and "where" that are not essentially connected with an action may sometimes aggravate its immorality. It's worse, e.g., to steal five dollars from a very poor person than it is to steal it from someone who is well off. It's a worse crime to kill a parent than a stranger. It is monstrous to rape a mother in the presence of her husband and children.

Motive and Intention

The other element required for insuring that an action is morally right is the agent's *motive,* why he or she is doing it. Helping an aged person across the street can be a morally right action unless the helper wants to maneuver that person into the path of a car or truck for some reason or other. It's one thing to administer pain relief to a person as an act of compassion but the same dose could be given with the motive of killing the patient. An otherwise good or morally right action performed from an evil motive is always morally wrong because an agent may never directly will evil, may never have an evil outcome as the object of his or her willing.

A good motive, on the other hand, will not make an intrinsically wrong action morally right--no matter how many good consequences it might produce. Murder is never justified, even if the murderer wants to save many lives by committing it. The end never justifies the means, i.e., the means to any end must be morally good; a good end will never make a morally bad means good.

Once again, I need to comment on the idea of *intention* taken in a different meaning from *motive*. I noted in an earlier chapter that intention can be taken to mean what we have decided to do, what we have set our will on accomplishing, acting on the belief of what state of affairs, consequences, our action will bring about. If we intend to do an action that is intrinsically wrong, that intention, even if we haven't actually acted on its, is immoral. It would be wrong as well to intend to do something which either circumstances or motive have made morally wrong.

Examples of Intrinsically Wrong Actions, Actions That Have Morality Built into Their Very Definitions

Suicide and Euthanasia

Our own lives are absolutely inviolable in the sense that there are never any situations that justify directly killing ourselves-even to alleviate intolerable pain or rid ourselves of poor quality of life. It follows that we may never help others take their own lives (a la Dr. Kevorkian in Michigan). Suicide and euthanasia are absolutely forbidden. We may, however, for a good reason, put ourselves in situations where our lives are in jeopardy. Soldiers going into battle risk being killed, but they don't directly intend, want their own deaths. (If they do intend or want them, they're committing suicide.)

Rape

Rape is so obviously a violation of the human person, so contrary to the meaning of human sexuality which requires a full and totally free commitment of one person to another, that it can never be justified. It's an action that *always* produces nothing but evil consequences; it is always wrong in its *object* no matter what the motive for it is or the good consequences it might (probably never) bring about.

Theft and Deceit

What belongs to another person is his or hers and we may not ordinarily take it against that person's will. I say "ordinarily" because ownership is not absolute: if, e.g., someone has more food than he or she needs and a starving person needs some of that food and can't get it any other way, it would be morally acceptable to take it from the owner's surplus--even against his or her will. The state, in the interest of the common good, may take a person's property for legitimate public use. Such actions are not *theft*.

It's always wrong to deceive another person when that person has a right to know the truth about a situation.

Slavery

To enslave someone is to take away the exercise of his or her autonomy, one of the most fundamental rights a person has. It removes most of a person's ability to make life plans, to find happiness according to his or her own interests and preferences. It violates human nature in such a fundamental way that it can never be justified.

Examples of Some Less Obviously Intrinsically Wrong Actions

There are some other actions that are seen as contrary to human well-being, less obviously in some cases than the one just discussed, perhaps, but nevertheless always forbidden on a *strong* reading of this version of natural law. Artificial contraception, sterilization, in-vitro fertilization, masturbation, and homosexual actions are among them. Some critics of natural-law moral theory claim that natural-law moralists mistakenly focus on human physiological "design" and functions, resort to "physicalism" when they argue that these actions are morally wrong. To illustrate what this challenge is all about, I'll discuss just one of them: artificial contraception. But before I get to that issue, I want to discuss an important moral principle used by natural-law moralists (and by some other moralists who don't follow that tradition) called "double effect."

The Principle of Double Effect

Sometimes, in the process of bringing about good, some good state of affairs, a good *effect,* we may also cause a bad, evil, effect right along with it. To justify this kind of action, we need to observe four conditions which make up what is known as the *principle of double effect:*

(1) The act being performed must be good in itself or at least morally indifferent, i.e., it may not be one of those intrinsically wrong actions we talked about earlier.

(2) The evil effect may not be used as the *means* to bring about the good effect we want to accomplish.

(3) We may never intend the evil effect in the sense that we desire it, that it is the *motive* for the act; only the good effect may be the object of our will, what we want.

Note that conditions (2) and (3) allow us to be *causally* responsible for a person's death, e.g., but *morally blameless* for bringing it about. As we discussed in an earlier chapter, it may seem puzzling to claim that we know we're going to kill someone, that we intend what our action will bring about, that it includes killing a person, but that we may not be blamed, morally speaking, for doing it. Another way of saying this is that we only *indirectly* intend the evil effect; it isn't our primary focus. The key here is that we have to exclude this effect from the effect we *want* to achieve, we must exclude it as an object of our willing. In effect, *knowing* what we will cause to happen does not entail *wanting* it to happen, does not explain *why* we're doing what we're doing.

(4) Finally, there must be a due proportion between the good and evil effects. Here's where consequences, after the three other conditions are met, become especially important: will the good state of affairs, the good effect, outweigh or at least equal in value the evil state of affairs caused by the action? If not, the action is forbidden.

To some extent, the moralist who uses double effect faces the same problem with this condition of the principle, weighing the good and bad effects, as the utilitarian moralist does. Just how does one go about deciding whether the good and bad effects are commensurate? Do property or money ever outweigh lives? When does the sheer number of people affected count in this calculation? Does the quality of the preferences of the people involved carry any weight, and, if so, how do we measure that?

Among the examples commonly used to illustrate how this principle is used are:

o Administering a potentially lethal dose of morphine which is the only way to alleviate a patient's unbearable pain;

o bombing an enemy installation knowing full well that some innocent civilians will be killed by the bombs;

o surgically removing a pregnant woman's cancerous uterus.

Let's examine each in a bit more detail just to better illustrate how the principle works.

The Morphine Case

The act of administering a drug to relieve intolerable pain (good effect) is a merciful act, *good in itself;* the agent *intends* only to relieve the pain, not the patient's death (evil effect). The patient's death is not the *means by which* the pain is alleviated, the morphine does that. There is a *due proportion* between alleviating this terrible suffering and the patient's unintended death. (Some people would quarrel with the idea that death and suffering are equivalent and would argue that the due proportion condition is not met in this case.)

Bombing an Enemy Installation

On the presumption that the bombing is part of self-defense in a just war to limit the enemy's potentially destructive power (good effect), the *act itself is morally good.* There is no *intention* to deliberately kill the innocent civilians (evil effect). The death of the civilians is not the *means by which* the good effect is realized. A *due proportion* is assumed between the deaths of the civilians and the destruction of the enemy's war-making resources.

The Cancerous Uterus

The pregnant woman's life is saved (good effect) by an action *good in itself* (surgery to remove the cancerous uterus). The death of her fetus (evil effect) is not *intended* and is not the *means by which* her life is saved. There is a *due proportion* between the two effects, weighing one life against the other.

Natural Law Theory's Strengths

The theory has several strengths for those persuaded by it. First, it provides an objective standard of right and wrong, namely, reason determining what is good and bad for human beings, judging what our nature requires to develop and flourish according to the full range of our intellectual, psychological, and biological capacities, what it takes for us to be "happy."

Since the fundamental essence of human nature is seen as the same for all men and women, the theory applies universally, everywhere, anytime.

The theory appeals to religious believers because of the idea that what reason commands us to do and avoid reflects what the eternal law of God, the Creator, commands as well.

Rights

Our contemporary understanding of human rights is based on the idea that human beings are individuals who are independent, free, and have a proprietary interest in their mental, spiritual, and intellectual capacities. Traditions prior to the "Enlightenment," including natural-law philosophers, understood rights in terms of the relationships among people that were derived from divine, natural, and positive law. I believe that natural law can support a whole host of human rights, rights that derive from a God-given nature and are not given by the constitutions or laws of any state, e.g., the right to:
o life;
o freedom to choose our life plans;
o education;
o marriage to a partner of our own choosing and the right to a marriage that is an exclusive sexual relationship between two partners committed to each other for life;
o have children;
o the kind of government we freely choose to live under;
o social and distributive justice, i.e., a fair share of the opportunities

and perquisites society has to offer;
o work or a profession that will allow us to earn a decent living and make a contribution to the welfare of our families and communities;
o resources to maintain our health.

As I noted earlier, none of these rights is given to us by the *state;* they are "natural," "human" rights. The state may regulate how we exercise them in the interest of the common good, to be sure that everyone's rights are respected by everybody else.   The state also provides, in some cases, the wherewithal to exercise those rights (e.g., education, help with the support of children, medical care).

Some Problematic Issues

In what follows, I will try to outline some of the difficulties that some natural-law moralists and moralists outside the tradition have with some of the specific conclusions derived from what I have been calling a strong interpretation of the theory. I will also try to show how the defenders of that interpretation might attempt to handle these challenges.

Intrinsically Wrong Actions

The theory is reasonably easy to apply at the very general levels of behavior (e.g., don't murder, steal, lie, rape, torture), but as life's situations get more and more complex it often becomes very difficult to decide just what actions really are or are not consistent with human excellence or well-being.

Many theorists have difficulty with the idea that some actions are always intrinsically wrong, that there is no set of circumstances that would ever justify doing them, that they may never be done no matter what the consequences of failing to do them might be. Suppose that a country at war with an unjust aggressor could save thousands of lives and stop the widespread destruction of cities and natural resources by directly killing the wives, children, and relatives of the enemy soldiers. Why wouldn't that be the morally right thing to do? Granted, at least for the sake of argument, that these victims are innocent civilians, not directly involved in their country's armed attacks, wouldn't their deaths be a small price to pay for all the good that would result, at least for the soldiers and the people of the country that was attacked unjustly? A utilitarian moralist might agree, after weighing all the potential good consequences involved, that it would, but the natural-law moralist would have to answer that the right of an innocent person is so fundamental to his or her well-being that it is *absolutely* inviolable; no situation can *ever* justify taking it directly, i.e., committing murder.

Note the use of the word "directly." In this context, it means that the agent intends the death of a person as a means to some end; that he or she *wants* that innocent person to die. As we saw in considering the principle of double effect, we are allowed to kill innocent human beings *indirectly*, in the sense that their deaths are not what we want to happen even if we cause them and as long as we're not using their deaths as the means to do what we want to get done. Their deaths are not the *object* of the action as is the case where an innocent person is directly killed. These victims may be innocent of any aggression towards us, but they may, unfortunately, be in the wrong place at the wrong time, living, e.g., near an enemy munitions plant targeted for destruction.

(The logic of what's happening to them, in the case of the war example, may, of course, escape the people being killed--especially if they happen to disagree with the war their leaders are pursuing. They might believe that their lives and the lives of their loved ones are inviolable and might resent the idea that they have been weighed in the due-proportion step of double effect and found to be of lesser value that the lives or property and freedom of the people responsible for killing them.)

Artificial Contraception: Assault on the Value of Conception?

I noted earlier that certain actions like artificial contraception, in-vitro fertilization, sterilization, masturbation, and homosexual actions are considered intrinsically wrong because they misuse natural faculties designed to serve human values; in effect, they are an attack on those values. Some moral philosophers challenge this argument because they consider it fallaciously founded on "physicalism," an illegitimate appeal to the natural design of physiological processes, on deriving moral conclusions from purely factual premises. I'll discuss just **one** of these actions, artificial contraception, to try to illustrate what this challenge is all about.

Suppose a wife and husband already have as many children as they can afford to support or that they feel psychologically incapable of rearing more children through the very difficult periods of late childhood and adolescence. It seems reasonable to many people for this couple to limit the size of their family by artificial means like "the pill."

The case looks even stronger in a situation where the wife has some serious health condition that might make a pregnancy dangerous.

Some people think that sterilization in the form of a vasectomy or tubal ligation could also be a legitimate means to limit conception. After all, we do all sorts of things to our bodies--up to and including amputating limbs and removing diseased organs--in the interest of our overall health and welfare. Even natural-law moralists agree that we may donate a kidney to save someone's life even though that violates the body's natural integrity. Vasectomy and tubal ligations are surgical procedures just like all these others; why aren't they also legitimate means to good human ends? What makes the moral difference?

Under the natural law's strong interpretation, the answer to using the pill or sterilization for contraception is that our bodily organs have explicit functions, are designed for certain very specific purposes oriented to a human good or value. While this may look like "physicalism," that charge is refuted by this emphasis on a *value* which eliminates any reliance on the purely physiological structure of these organs as grounds for moral judgment about their use.

The human reproductive system is a case in point. Sexual intercourse has two equally valuable purposes: fostering the mutual love and unity of two people exclusively committed to each other, and conceiving children. Artificial devices like the pill, condoms, or spermicides are direct barriers to the potential union of sperm and ovum, and by directly interfering with this purpose of sexual intercourse attack a *value* nature's order is directed to.

The same is true for contraceptive sterilization, a process that differs from amputations and removing diseased organs because in these cases, a life-threatening condition is eliminated; there is no direct interference with or any intention to interfere with an organ's natural physiological processes. When a healthy kidney is transplanted, its valuable function is not destroyed; it will continue, hopefully, to operate as nature designed it-even though it's in some other person's body. It serves the value of *life*.

Sex Without Conception: When Is It Morally Legitimate?

A key principle cited against artificial contraception is that "every act of intercourse must be open to conception." In its most restrictive sense, it would mean that intercourse is morally legitimate *only when the physical conditions for conception are present*. But even the moralists who favor a strong interpretation of natural law do not understand "openness to conception" that literally. There are situations where conception isn't possible because of natural or accidental sterility, yet intercourse is morally justified because it serves its other value: the reinforcement, the deepening, of the couple's mutual love and unity. Here are some examples:

o *Natural family planning:* Natural-law moralists agree that a couple may have good reasons for limiting their family's size or even for not having children at all, e.g.., those mentioned earlier: family economics, psychological limitations of the parents, the woman's health. It is perfectly legitimate for them to take advantage of the woman's natural fertility cycle and have intercourse during non-fertile times; they are not deliberately and directly attacking the value of conception since it is nature itself that makes conception impossible.

o *Sterility:* Couples who are sterile for any reason whatever may make love. In the case where the wife has had a radical hysterectomy, e.g., there is obviously no way conception can occur. A husband's sperm count may be so low that conception is extremely unlikely. A woman may even take the pill to regulate her menstrual cycle, making herself sterile for some period of time. In this case, she doesn't directly intend the sterility; she intends only to regulate her cycle. The principle of double effect makes her action morally licit.

o *The danger of rape:* The act of "taking the pill" is not morally wrong in itself, as we have just seen. Using the pill (or any other "barrier" method to prevent conception) is a morally legitimate option for a woman at high risk of being raped. The crucial moral point that is made in this situation is that she is not participating voluntarily in the act of rape, whereas a couple using the same methods is having sex voluntarily.

Does the Object of the Act Where Natural or Artificial Sterility Is Present Differ from the Object of the Act of Artificial Contraception?

Whether an act is intrinsically wrong depends, as we saw earlier, on its object. In a case where the act of intercourse is not open to conception because of natural or accidental sterility, it is not wrong to intend an ejaculation of sperm that will knowingly be ineffective as far as conception is concerned. The object of the act, after its consequences, circumstances, and intention have been collapsed into its description, is, in these cases, fostering mutual love and unity; that gives it its proper *moral* description, just like collapsing the consequences, circumstances, and intention into the physical act of killing determines whether it is murder of self-defense. The physiological process of orgasm is an integral part of the act of *love* in these situations; it serves a significant human value.

This judgment rests on what is naturally given, i.e., we may use natural situations--whether arising from ordinary biological processes (e.g., no conception possible outside the fertile period or during pregnancy, natural sterility) or even from surgical sterilization done for reasons of health (e.g, removing a cancerous uterus or cancerous ovaries).

Is the object of the act of intercourse where artificial contraception is used significantly different, morally speaking, from the act of intercourse in these other situations? The motives of couples using artificial contraception are the same as the motives of couples using natural family planning or who are sterile for some other reason. It could be argued that just as we may kill another human being, directly act against the most fundamental human value of preserving one's existence, for a good reason, it would seem that a good reason should allow a couple to act against one value, statistically probable conception, while fostering the other equal value of human sexuality: deepening their love for each other. Although the use of the pill or other type of barrier birth control method might look like an attack on the value of conception, these methods appear to some moralists as simply using human reason and the knowledge of human physiology to regulate natural processes in the interest of the other equally valuable end of intercourse as well as other values like economic stability of the family, proper parental attention to the growth and development of children the couple may already have, or the mother's health, for instance. This does not entail that a couple has no use for the value of a conception that only *might* occur (although that might be the motivation for some couples); they are not misusing a natural faculty for an unnatural end. On the contrary, they are using it to promote one of its own natural ends, a positive value along with, in many cases, other "family" values.

The strong interpretation of natural law answers this argument by pointing out that the additional circumstances of doing something to intentionally prevent conception interferes with, *violates,* the design of a natural function, misuses a faculty by opposing its natural end, and, therefore, must be regarded as an attack on the value that function is supposed to serve. The official teaching of the Catholic Church, e.g., hinges precisely on this point: all that is needed to distinguish, morally speaking, the object of the act of intercourse where natural or accidental sterility is involved from the act of intercourse using artificial contraception is *the direct and deliberate introduction of a barrier to conception.*

Abortifacients Used for Birth Control

It's important to note that the use of techniques like the pill or spermicides has to be contrasted with those that are abortifacient, i.e, that kill a fertilized ovum or prevent it from being implanted in the uterus. The issue here, of course, is that these zygotes are already thought to be human beings with full moral status: persons; in that case, it follows that directly killing them (preventing implantation in the uterus is seen as a direct act of killing) is murder.

Condoms and Aids

Linked to the artificial contraception issue is the controversy over
using condoms to prevent the transmission of AIDS to a sexual
partner. A common objection made by some natural-law moralists is
that their use will encourage both heterosexual and homosexual
promiscuity. More fundamentally, however, not only are these actions
at issue when condoms are used, there is also the high probability that
in the case of heterosexual partners, condoms will prevent conception.

With regard to the issue of the condom as a contraceptive device, it's
a question of whether the use of a condom is always, necessarily,
morally wrong even though it may keep a sperm from uniting with an
ovum. It may be that the principle of double effect could be used to
show that it isn't.

Take the case of a husband or wife who has become infected with
the AIDS virus through a blood transfusion or, in a health-care
situation, from an accidental stick with a needle tainted by blood from
an AIDS-infected person. Why would it be wrong for this couple to
use condoms to protect the uninfected partner? It can be argued that
using a condom is not intrinsically wrong; as was pointed out earlier,
intending an ejaculation that can't be effective does not always seem
wrong in its object. Its final, full moral specification has to depend on
consequences, circumstances, and motive. The couple only directly
intends the value of promoting their love and unity. To want to
prevent conception is one thing, but to want and intend to prevent a
life-threatening infection from being transmitted to a person's spouse
is quite another. Granted, conception may also be prevented, but only
as an unwanted, indirectly intended effect of what seems to be, given
the elements of consequences, circumstances, motive and intention, a
morally good action. Some natural-law ethicists could very well see
this situation as a clear-cut example of the double-effect principle at
work.

Natural Law and Virtue

St. Thomas held that just knowing how to distinguish morally right
actions from wrong ones is not enough to lead a moral life. We have
to perform morally right actions habitually, from a morally good

character, i.e., we have to practice *virtue*. I'll talk about the concept of virtue in a subsequent chapter.

Chapter 8

Immanuel Kant: Pure Practical Reason

Consequences Don't Count

The utilitarian and natural-law moral philosophers we discussed argued that we have to consider the consequences of our actions when we make our moral judgments. Utilitarians make them the ultimate criterion for deciding right and wrong; proponents of natural law believe that while consequences are not the ultimate criterion of moral judgment, they do play a part in determining what kind of action, morally speaking, we are dealing with.

I will now briefly describe the approach to moral theory proposed by Immanuel Kant (1724-1804), who believed that consequences don't count at all in making moral judgments, that reason alone lays down the moral law.

Having a Good Will

Kant claimed that the only thing in the world that can be good without qualification of any kind is a "good will," one that is good only because the person who has one desires to do his or her duty, to act solely "from duty." A person's will isn't good just because his or her actions along with their consequences are good.   Someone might perform a good action like helping a person who is in need, but that by itself wouldn't give the action *moral worth*. He or she might have done the good deed just for a reward or to get some kind of public recognition. The point, for Kant, is: *why* is the person acting that way? For the act to be morally worthy, it must be done purely from the motive, the desire, to do one's duty, to always act out of respect for the moral law. Just what is the moral law?

The Moral Law

To understand what Kant is getting at, we have to first examine his distinction between two types of imperatives, commands, that reason generates: hypothetical and categorical.

A *hypothetical* imperative tells us what we have to do if we want to accomplish something. If, e.g., we want to become a champion athlete, we have to practice and train for the sport or sports we want to excel in. If we want to be a nurse or CPA, we have to study that profession and be certified by the state in which we want to practice. Notice that the steps we have to take (the imperative) are conditional on what we want to accomplish. That's what makes these imperatives hypothetical: They bind us only *if* we want to satisfy a particular desire. To eliminate the imperative, to be free of it, we simply eliminate the desire we want to satisfy. Since Kant didn't believe that desires (except the desire to act from duty) play any part in making moral judgments, he had to eliminate hypothetical imperatives as a basis for the moral law.

A *categorical* imperative, by contrast, doesn't require any kind of condition in order to bind us; it obliges *absolutely,* with no exceptions. Once acknowledged, we can't get rid of it like we can a hypothetical imperative. Only a categorical imperative can possibly bind us morally because it does not depend on satisfying desires and inclinations. Kant believed that there was only one categorical imperative:

> Act only on a maxim by which you can will that it, at the same time, should become a general law.

What Kant meant by the word "general" in this formula is that the maxim in question has to be made universal, binding on everybody, everywhere, all the time, and, as such, is *natural* and must be willed as a general law of nature.

Maxims of Actions

How do we make sense of Kant's somewhat torturous formulation of the moral law? First, we have to understand what he meant by a *maxim*. A maxim is a principle or rule that serves as a guide to performing an action. Kant himself provided several theoretical examples to illustrate what he was getting at. I'll try to simplify a couple of them.

Suppose you want to borrow money but know that you can't pay it back. Would it be morally right to promise the lender that you will pay it back knowing full well that you never can? According to Kant, we'd first have to look at the maxim governing this action, namely: "whenever I want to borrow money, I will promise to pay it back even though I know I never will." Could this maxim be made a general law of nature that everybody could abide by? Of course not, Kant argued; no one could ever will that this maxim be made universal. On the one hand, the person using this maxim would want everybody to live up to the promise of repaying borrowed money (if the practice of lending money were to continue as a useful social instrument); on the other, he or she would want to be made an exception: in effect, not want the practice to be observed universally. To try to make this exception would be inconsistent with what the practice requires: i.e., *everybody has to observe it all the time.* Such an attempt would be *rationally incoherent,* a contradiction in one's will.

Another of Kant's examples: suppose that you didn't want to put yourself out to help others in need; you just didn't want to be bothered with these people. Could you generalize this line of thinking as a universal maxim, something like: "let everybody get along as well as they can; I won't hinder or help them." No, Kant said; you yourself might need help some day, and you wouldn't want others to be bound by this maxim. In effect, if you tried to will this as a general maxim, you would generate a contradiction in your will by excluding yourself from the generalization process.

Note that, without attempting a long explanation of the notion of contradiction and irrationality involved in Kant's theory of generalizing maxims, the key here for him is *reason.* Reason dictates what may or may not be done; when reason detects a contradiction in the attempt to formulate a maxim into a law for everybody, it forbids the action that is based on that maxim; it would be morally wrong to do it. Even though Kant's own examples of maxims look suspiciously like they depend on consequences, i.e., "what would happen if everybody did that," (sounds like rule utilitarianism, doesn't it?) the thrust of what he means turns, in the final analysis, on the idea of irrationality, on an incoherence in trying to universalize one's maxim.

Most people encountering Kant's approach to morality find it extremely harsh. Take, e.g., lying. Kant argued that we must *never* lie; we could never universalize the maxim: "always lie when it is to your advantage," because nobody would ever trust anybody else's word. Kant believed that even if a murderer came to your door asking whether his intended victim was in your house, and the victim was in fact there, you would have to tell the murderer the truth.

This apparently bizarre conclusion has led some philosophers to point out that Kant's process of universalizing maxims is, in the case of lying, e.g., too narrow in its scope. Why couldn't we universalize the maxim that we should always tell a lie when it would save somebody from an unjust assailant? What contradiction or inconsistency could that possibly generate?

A Kingdom of Ends

Kant had another formulation of the categorical imperative which he claimed was equivalent to the one we just discussed. This one seems to be more palatable as a moral principle. It holds that rational beings, precisely because they are rational and autonomous, are persons who have intrinsic value, dignity; in our dealing with each other we must always treat each other as valuable, as ends, and never use others only as a means to satisfy our own purposes. We have a duty to treat others with respect. This duty is not based on inclination, feelings, impulses, or the effect our actions may have on others but is a law dictated by reason. We simply recognize that all of us are fellow citizens in a kingdom of ends, valuable for our own sakes, united in a system of common laws. Each of us is a sovereign, an autonomous lawgiver in that kingdom, subservient to his or her own lawmaking. That very autonomy is, for Kant, the foundation of our human dignity which we may never violate by our actions, no matter how much good they may bring about.

Kinds of Duties

Kant believed that there are two classes of duties: perfect and imperfect. Perfect duties demand, e.g., that we keep promises and observe what justice and respect for human dignity require. There are no exceptions to fulfilling these duties--no matter how much we might be inclined by our desires and preferences to ignore them. Imperfect duties like duties of virtue, e.g., "self perfection, " are not binding in the same way that perfect duties are. We have a duty to the happiness of others, but we don't have a duty to sacrifice ourselves for them.

Chapter 9

Rights

What Is a Right?

Thomas Jefferson insisted, in the Declaration of Independence, that we are endowed by our Creator with "unalienable" rights, among which are life, liberty, and the pursuit of happiness. The Constitution of the United States includes a Bill of Rights that limits the actions the Government may take against its citizens. The United Nations has published a *Universal Declaration of Human Rights* to which human rights activists often appeal in condemning governments for their unjust treatment of their people. Anyone who watches American TV crime shows knows that the police must read people they have arrested their rights. We all take for granted that we have certain rights that no individual, group, or government is supposed to violate.

The concept of a "right" turns out to be quite complex, and a good many articles and books have been written to explain it. It's an extremely important moral notion because it helps establish important boundaries between the individual and the communities he or she is part of. I propose, for my purposes here, to briefly describe some of the issues and questions philosophers have raised about the meaning of a right.

Some examples of rights we commonly believe we have:

o The right to life;

o to choose a career, a life's work;

o to equal opportunity in education, employment, career advancement, housing, and access to political offices and positions;

o to practice a religion, to live by a set of religious beliefs;

o to marry whom we please and to have a family;

o to decide how we will be governed;

o to physical and psychological integrity, e.g., not to be assaulted or tortured;

o to privacy in our personal lives;

o to use a share of the world's natural resources to preserve and enhance our lives and the lives of those who depend on us;

o to move freely about in the world;

o to protection and other benefits afforded by our government;

o to support and education by our parents and society;

o to fair dealings in the marketplace;

o to fair compensation for the work others have agreed to pay us for.

It's simple enough to make a list of our rights, but the concept itself of just what a right is is highly abstract. A right is obviously not attached in some way to any physical characteristic of human beings that we can point to; it's not even a psychological trait like intelligence that we might identify by devising some sort of empirical test for it.

Philosophers and legal experts have offered different definitions or descriptions of what a right is. I'll examine some of the major ones.

Rights as Claims

One approach to understanding what a right is is to see it as a "claim" someone makes, e.g., to a particular kind of treatment by others. The last four examples of the rights on the list just offered are *positive* claims made on others. If, e.g., someone threatens to assault us, the police have to protect us. If we meet the conditions specified for receiving social security payments, the government must pay us on schedule. If we have children, we are obliged to educate them, and society has to provide school systems to help us meet this obligation. Merchants are obliged to hand over the items we buy from them. Employers have to pay us what they promised to pay for our work.

In addition to the positive claims we make on others, we also expect that they will not interfere with actions we are performing or want to perform. This expectation is also a kind of claim, an insistence that no one may restrict our liberty unless the exercise of that liberty will conflict with someone else's legitimate, overriding claim. In this sense, it is a "negative" right. I believe that all but the last four of the examples provided on my list fall into this category.

An important point to make about claims is that it's never enough to simply make one; there must be a justification, a rationale, for asserting it.

Rights as Entitlements Based on Interests

Another way to think about rights is to see them as entitlements following from the need to satisfy our *interests,* but we have to be careful here; we need to offer some reason or reasons that establish an interest as an entitlement. I'm interested, e.g., in collecting my duly-earned wages from my employer and I'm entitled to them, I have a right to them. I may, however, have an interest in winning the lottery, but that interest, by itself, obviously doesn't establish a claim to winning it.

Rights as Powers

Some philosophers think a right is a physical or psychological power over others that forces them to do something or provide something to somebody else. Tyrants, of course have that kind of power, but something more is needed to turn power over others into a right over them, namely, a justification or authorization for exercising that power. It's also evident that a person may be powerless to enforce his or her claims, but those claims may still be valid; so it seems overly simplistic to identify a right with a physical or psychological power as such.

Other philosophers have held that the natural moral law confers power on us, i.e., if nature has endowed us, by virtue of the kind of beings we are, with the power to act or to acquire and posses something, we may assert a claim to act that way or obtain that something, we have a "right" to it. An example might be using natural resources: We need them to survive and live a decent human life and we have the ability to access them, so we have a claim to some fair share of them, a right to access them. In this case, however, we have a justification for the use of a power--which says more than that we simply have the power; we have a warrant for exercising it. So, it again seems clear that just having the power isn't enough by itself;

something else is needed before its use can be established as a right.

Claims, Interests, and Power Taken Together

Perhaps the notions of claims, interests, and power can be used together to provide part of the definition of what a right is rather than using any one of them as the whole definition. Let's try defining a right as a power a person has:
o to assert immunity from interference by any individual, group, or government with respect to possessing some material good or to an action in his or her own interest;
o to assert that some individual, group, or government is obliged to act positively on his or her behalf.

Justifying Rights: Where Do They Come from?

It should be clear from our considerations so far that when we assert our rights, we expect the individuals, groups, or governments to whom we address them to honor them because they are legitimate, are warranted by some acceptable reason or set of reasons. This idea of a justification has to be understood as any complete definition of a right. That leads us to ask what an acceptable justification might be based on. In short, we need to know where rights come from.

Some rights appear to belong to us *naturally,* simply from our human nature which we recognize as having fundamental value and concomitant dignity that empowers us to assert demands which must be honored by others. Rights like the right to life, to use a fair share of natural resources, to education, marriage and a family, religious freedom, free movement about the world, a government of our own choosing, and freedom of speech are examples of natural rights. No government gives them to us; they are ours simply because we are human beings who are valuable and have dignity. Governments may regulate how we exercise these rights in the interest of safeguarding the exercise of these same rights by others, but government doe not give them to us.

Some rights are *legal* entitlements: they are established by legitimate governments for the common good and may be enforced and rescinded by government. Several common examples that come to mind are unemployment compensation, social security and welfare benefits, and particular forms of police protection. Governments also establish judicial forums for the remedy of crimes and torts committed against people and for the enforcement of contracts. Government agencies see to it that we are afforded equal opportunity in education and employment.

Some philosophers have argued that rights are interests upheld by the law, that without the notion of legal sanctions for violating those interests, the whole notion of a right is meaningless. Natural rights, however, don't seem to require the idea of legal sanctions before they are recognized as rights; the rights to life and liberty are conspicuous examples. We have these rights, we think, regardless of whether or not there is a government to enforce sanctions against their violation. They belong to us in virtue of our human nature.

There are those philosophers who have held that the concept of a right is meaningless without the concept of a correlative duty on the part of someone toward the holder of a right. This is easy to understand in the case of positive rights: If I have a right, for example, to a salary from my employer, her or she has a duty to pay me. If a child has a right to care and education from its parents, the parents have a duty to provide them. If I make a contract with another party, that party has a positive claim on me based on the terms of the contract. It does seem clear that wherever we find a duty, there is someone to whom that duty is owed, someone who has a corresponding claim to what is owed.

In the case of negative rights, however, the idea of correlative duties seems a little more problematical. Does, e.g., my right to move freely about entail that every human being in the world has a duty not to interfere with my movement? Do I have a duty not to get in the way of every human being moving about in Calcutta? In some sense, that is true, of course; if I'm physically in Calcutta I may not, without some clear justification, stop anybody else from moving about in that city. So I have a duty then and there not to interfere with that person's movement, but it seems strange that everybody has a duty, except in the conditional sense just offered, to refrain from getting in the way of everybody else in the world. The same thinking seems to apply to all other negative rights.

As you can see from this brief sketch, there are many questions that can be raised about the meaning and extent of a right. We are all sure that we have rights; it's just hard to give an easy account of what it means to have them.

Chapter 10

Virtue

What Is a Virtue?

Who is a virtuous person? One who is kind, benevolent, loving, generous, loyal, patriotic, witty, courageous, prudent, just, friendly, temperate, modest, trustworthy-and on and on. We think of virtues as good character traits. They are good because they contribute to an individual's well-being and that of others. They have to do with character because the actions they give rise to come from the kind of person an agent is.

While we have many innate physical and mental capacities, we can't consistently accomplish anything with them while they're in their "raw" state, so to speak; moving from the capability of doing something to doing it well involves a lot of hard work. The polished performer operates from habit developed by long hours of the repeated activity needed to achieve and maintain a particular skill. To paraphrase an old joke: the only way to get to Carnegie Hall is by practice, practice, practice. Once acquired, habits allow us to act with the ease born of proficiency.

The same is true of virtue. A virtue is a good habit. Someone who performs a single "virtuous" act doesn't necessarily have the virtue it is related to; for that, he or she has to do it *habitually*. I might give a large donation to a friend's charitable cause just to leave a good impression of myself; but unless I make charitable contributions on some regular basis, it's not likely that I'm really a generous person.

Philosophers on Virtue

Philosophers have a long history of thinking about virtue. Here is a brief sample of what some of them had to say about it.

Socrates thought that virtue was knowledge; he believed that we wouldn't do anything wrong if we knew it was wrong to begin with.

Plato believed that virtues (excellences) were needed to control the three parts of the soul: the rational, spirited (a sort of police-like element that could curb desires and be guided by reason), and appetitive. Wisdom allows us to reason correctly; courage helps the spirited element control our appetites; temperance helps us use our appetites in moderation. The virtuous person is a just person: One in whom all these elements are harmoniously balanced.

Aristotle believed that human happiness was bound up with our need for activity; for constantly striving toward the *good,* toward ends, goals, set within a framework of social purposes and interactions among the members of a community and the various roles people have there. Only when we seek these ends and pursue these roles rationally and with ease, habitually, *virtuously,* can we be happy. Moreover, these virtuous activities have to recur over a lifetime to insure real happiness. How does one become virtuous in Aristotle's scheme? By doing virtuous acts: We become just by acting justly; temperate, by acting temperately; truthful, by telling the truth consistently.

Aristotle also thought that having "external" goods, wealth, was a condition of leading a virtuous life; a person who was poverty-stricken for most of his or her life, e.g., could not practice virtue. Slaves who didn't have wealth of their own and weren't free to choose their activities, their "life-style," couldn't lead a virtuous life.

St. Thomas Aquinas, following St. Augustine, called a virtue a habit of the mind which perfects our capacities, the powers of our human nature, and enables them to perform right actions perfectly.

The stoics thought that virtue was its own reward, happiness itself. They based that belief on our knowledge that nature operates under inexorable laws which we have to live with. Virtue makes us resigned to what nature does to us. We need to control our emotions in the face of what happens to us, good and bad; in a word, we have to learn to live with our fate. When we are indifferent to what fate hands out to us, we are virtuous, and that alone is what makes us happy.

David Hume, an eighteenth-century philosopher, argued that the virtues are really to be found in human sentiments, in our emotions and attitudes. The most important virtue for him was benevolence, a habitual attitude of goodwill toward others and their interests. Certain other virtues are "artificial," i.e., they depend on rules established by society so that people can live together peaceably. Justice, e.g., is just such a virtue. We realize that we have to treat each other justly, and that means following certain rules society has laid down, e.g., for property transactions. Reason is related to these artificial virtues in that it tells us how to implement these rules impartially.

Some thinkers, e.g., utilitarians, see the virtues simply as dispositions needed to produce good consequences. Others, like Hume in the case of the artificial virtues, argue that virtue is just a disposition to act in accordance with rules. In effect, for these people, virtues are just means to ends.

Some Questions About Virtue Theory

It's clear that philosophers have different ideas about what the precise definition of virtue is, but they all seem to agree that a virtue is a habit, a disposition to act, a quality a person has developed through learning or practice. As we try to better understand what habits are of interest to moral philosophers, we'll raise some questions and, as we go along, try to develop some answers to them:

(1) What is the difference between a skill and a virtue? Are all habits that are associated with a person's good character necessarily *moral* habits, moral virtues?

(2) Is an action morally right because it is virtuous or are actions virtuous because they are morally right in the first place and have become habitual, part of a person's character?

(3) Is the proper focus of moral philosophy identifying which habits make up moral character or is its job to derive and justify principles and rules from a moral theory like utilitarianism, natural law, or Kantian rationalism? Or, perhaps, is it supposed to do both?

Let's begin by looking at some of the habits selected philosophers have called virtues.

The Traditional Virtues

Here are four traditional virtues that go back as far as Plato. For Plato and Aristotle, the meaning of the word "virtue" is "excellence" in the sense of perfectly fulfilling a function. In today's terminology, it is probably closer to our concept of doing things well, proficiently.

These virtues are called "cardinal" by some ethicists because they believe that all the other virtues "hinge" ("cardo" is the Latin word for "hinge") on having these four; no one can be virtuous unless he or she has them. Here they are:

o *Prudence,* which identifies for us the appropriate means to the ends, the aims we seek, and prompts us to use those means. Since choosing among means to ends is a rational process, prudence is considered to be an "intellectual" and "practical" virtue rather than a moral virtue which is concerned with controlling actions, appetites, and emotions. St. Thomas Aquinas claimed that prudence helps us find the truly human good in particular actions.

Some philosophers claim that prudence is acquired by instruction and learning from experience rather than practice because it is a function of the intellect, not of appetite. Some have argued that none of the virtues can function without prudence. It is required, e.g., by the doctrine of the *mean,* most notably proposed by Aristotle, which holds that every virtuous action has a "middle way," and any habitual deviation to either side of that way results in a vice. (I'll examine his doctrine of the "mean" in a little more detail later.)

o *Justice,* a virtue concerned with our actions toward others. Somewhat simplistically, it means the willingness to give to others what is due to them. It inclines buyers and sellers, e.g., to abide by the terms of their bargains and be willing to live up to them ("commutative" justice) and obliges a society to distribute its rewards, perquisites and offices equitably among its members ("distributive" and "social" justice).

o *Fortitude,* which inclines us to act courageously in the face of hardship, danger, or death.

o *Temperance,* which acts as a curb on our appetite for sensible pleasure.

Justice, fortitude, and temperance are considered to be moral virtues acquired by repeating just, courageous, and temperate actions.

Here are just a few examples of other virtues identified by philosophers:

o liberality (munificence, generosity),

o magnanimity,

o chastity,

o friendship,

o truthfulness (the willingness to express ourselves openly and honestly to others),

o good cheer, affability,

o eutrapeleia (cheering up others by communicating our own cheerful feelings and attitudes to others,

o constancy,

o industry,

o philotomia (proper ambition for honor),

o gracefulness,

o tact,

o reliability,

o loyalty.

In every case, these virtues are good habits that are part of the character of the person who has them.

Aristotle's Doctrine of the Mean

The Greek word Plato and Aristotle used for "virtue" was "arete," which is more properly translated as an "excellence," the ability to act or perform a function well. For these two philosophers, all excellences of the personality are virtues. They did differentiate the intellectual virtue of prudence, practical wisdom ("phronesis") from a person's other virtues because it is an intellectual virtue that is not acquired by repeating prudential acts; as noted earlier, one becomes prudent by instruction and learning from experience. The *moral* virtues, however, are acquired by repeating the acts they are associated with and are characterized by their function of controlling actions, desires (e.g., for food, drink, or sex), and emotions (e.g., love, pity, anger).

Aristotle made a significant contribution to the understanding of what virtues are through his famous doctrine of the "mean," his idea that virtuous conduct lies "midway" between a defect and an excess in an activity. To illustrate what he had in mind, consider these virtues:

o *Fortitude:* The courageous person does not endanger himself or herself rashly, nor is he or she a coward. True courage lies somewhere in between these two extremes. We need the intellectual virtue of prudence to tell us just where, in any concrete situation calling for courage, that middle ground lies. The same is true for all virtues; prudence shows us where the mean lies; it is prudence that brings actions into conformity with reason.

o *Temperance:* This is a virtue that keeps a person from drinking or eating too much or not enough; it keeps the sexual appetite from turning into lust (excess) or sexual insensitivity (defect).

o *Generosity:* The generous person must be careful to avoid prodigality on the one hand and stinginess on the other.

o *Righteous anger:* A person must control his or her anger, avoiding irrational anger, too much anger relative to a situation calling for righteous indignation, and the failure to get angry at all in relevant circumstances.

The "Mean" Is a Relative Notion

It's important to understand that the mean is always relative to the individual person. One person's foolhardiness may turn out to be another's courageous act. A 110-lb., short person should probably not stand up to a 250-lb., six-foot, four-inch world-class wrestler; but another wrestler of equal stature might well do so. What might be gluttony for one person might be just enough of a meal for another.

What Makes an Action Morally Right?

Does Aristotle's doctrine of the mean entail that actions are morally right precisely because we can find the middle way in them, because they are virtuous, or are actions really virtuous because they are morally right in the first place, i.e., they conform to a standard of right action provided by a moral theory, and then, while also satisfying the "middle way," spring from a personality habituated to perform them when they are called for?

It's doubtful that Aristotle thought that an action is virtuous solely because a mean can be found in it; rather, since it is in accord with reason, it will necessarily have a middle way. Aristotle thought that there were some actions that could never be virtuous because there simply is no middle way in them: e.g., adultery, theft, and murder. It isn't an excess or deficiency in these actions that makes them vices; they are simply bad *in themselves*. The idea that there could be just enough adultery or stealing or murder made no sense to him.

What is it, then, that makes an action in accord with reason? Certainly prudence has a role to play here, but just how does it function? Is it the case that we have to first examine an action and "prudently" decide whether it is morally right or at least morally indifferent in the light of some moral theory before we can decide what would constitute a mean or an excess or defect in performing it, what would make it virtuous or vicious?

How this question is answered bears on a current controversy over whether moral philosophers have incorrectly focused on moral theory and ignored the importance of virtue theory, the fundamental issue of moral character. Before attempting to crystallize some ideas about how this controversy should be resolved, I want to discuss some more fundamental questions about the nature of moral virtue.

Moral Habits and Habits That Are Skills or "Nice" Qualities of Character

Since the habits that should interest moralists are those that make up a morally good character, it seems reasonable to ask whether all skills or "nice" traits, excellences, are necessarily moral ones. It doesn't seem obvious that just acting or performing a function well entails acting virtuously, at least in the way we usually think of moral virtue. Some habits, like skills, really are just "excellences," and even though they dispose a person to act well and even contribute in some way to his or her own good and the well-being of others, it seems strange to think of them as "moral."

A star quarterback on a football team, e.g., may consistently, habitually, throw unerring passes with the greatest of ease to the delight of himself and his fans, but that skill as such has nothing to do with his moral character. An artist may practice his or her craft with exceptional skill born of years of training and experience, or a brilliant scholar may demonstrate exceptional habits of concentration and perseverance in researching his or her chosen field, yet these qualities do not insure that either of them is a morally virtuous person.

Just what is it, then, that distinguishes a moral virtue from a simple skill, the ability to do something consistently well or even from a pleasant, "nice," personality trait?

One difference between a skill and a moral virtue is that a person who has certain skills is not obliged to practice them all the time, but it's never all right for a person to fail to exercise a moral virtue in a situation that calls for it. I may opt not to play my musical instrument, e.g., as long as there is no special obligation for me to do so (like being paid for a virtuoso performance), but I may not fail to act generously or courageously or honestly in a relevant set of circumstances where a significant human interest is at stake.

There seems to be a clear difference between a moral virtue and certain personality traits. Some people may be witty, affable, and charming, but that doesn't entail that they are morally virtuous. Scoundrels may go about working their scams wittily, affably, and with charm, but they're still scoundrels.

Another way to differentiate skill and desirable personality traits from moral virtues is to examine the actions they generate. If we examine actions in the light of a moral theory like utilitarianism, Kant's pure practical reason, or natural law with a view to determining whether these actions are morally right or wrong, we may then conclude that the habits, the dispositions to repeat those actions we decide are morally right, are *moral* virtues. Other habits that are nice personality traits might be might be useful to our social life, might help to make our relationships with others congenial, and certainly would be nice qualities to have. They would make us more generally likable or even lovable, but might or might not be morally virtuous depending on the motives from which they were done-e.g., out of love or respect for the dignity of others. Social manners like ordinary politeness, dressing appropriately for social functions, refraining from vulgar language in the presence of children, respect for people holding political or religious offices, and deference to the aged or infirm come to mind. A person might demonstrate these kinds of qualities regularly (habitually), but only to get ahead in his or her profession or to get elected to some political office, but we would hardly be willing to call him or her "virtuous" in that respect.

All of these traits certainly are "good" for the people they affect, but that by itself doesn't make them moral traits. The key reason why it doesn't seems to be that the interactions they are concerned with are not necessarily subject to moral analysis, i.e., a judgment about their moral rightness or wrongness.   I may have a moral obligation to respect certain rights of others (e.g., not to trespass on their property), but that doesn't seem to include being polite to them as I do so. A gas station attendant is not required, morally speaking, to pump my gas and wash my windshield "affably." If he or she does, it may make our transaction more pleasant, but there are no moral overtones necessarily associated with it.

To the extent, however, that impoliteness or lack of deference or observing some social custom turns out to be deliberately harmful to someone (it might be done out of spite or the desire to cause emotional distress), we would surely think it was morally wrong.

It also seems true that having a virtuous character does not entail having nice personal qualities. There may be people, e.g., who are just, temperate, and courageous without being affable or witty or charming in their relations with others. We might see them as "cold fish" or even puritanical, but it wouldn't seem correct to say they are not virtuous.

Pseudo-Virtue?

It appears that people can have certain habits we ordinarily think of as moral virtues but, depending on the situation in which they are exercised, aren't moral at all. Courage, for instance, which helps us face hardship and danger, is a case in point. A boxer facing an opponent in the ring may exhibit great courage in standing up to the blows and pains he or she is about to suffer, but that show of fortitude doesn't have to be described as moral. A bank robber aware of the possibility of being arrested or even shot by the police may carry on courageously with his or her crime, but certainly wouldn't earn a commendation for being stalwart in the face of danger. Soldiers may show exceptional bravery while fighting in a war they know is unjust or disproportionately destructive of human life and property. It might even be the case that the courage shown in all these examples is exercised prudently, neither in a cowardly or foolhardy manner, yet it still doesn't deserve to be called "moral" since it is in the service of a morally questionable activity.

A person, though, who habitually overcomes temptations to lie or steal or commit some injustice, shows the kind of courage we would commonly call "moral." So, it seems that we have the beginning of an answer to the question of whether an action is morally right because it is virtuous or virtuous because it is morally right and performed habitually, virtuously, in the proper set of circumstances. In the case of the examples just described, the kind of action and the motives and results for which a person acts seem to be critical for first determining whether what he or she is doing is morally right and, if so, for concluding that the habit that prompted that action is morally good, virtuous.

Virtue Theory or Moral Theory?

We should now be able to address more intelligently the question of whether virtue theory or moral theories of right action are the proper focus of moral philosophy.

Some philosophers argue that different moral theories like those we examined earlier are so controversial or so defective in some way that any reasonable person will despair of ever determining which of them offers the best approach to resolving moral controversies. The only solution is to resort to virtue theory. In effect, an action is the morally right thing to do or avoid because it is something a virtuous person--e.g, courageous, loyal, just, honest, temperate, truthful, etc.--would do or avoid.

There is one key difficulty with this view that I propose to consider and that has to do with *knowledge:* how do we *know* that what we are doing is virtuous to begin with?

We can't rely on cultural relativism, i.e., by appealing to the fact that our society or group considers a particular action done habitually a virtuous one. We've already addressed the pitfalls associated with cultural relativism: e.g., the very same action that is considered right or virtuous in one culture may be seen as immoral and vicious in another. If cultural relativism is true, we have no way of deciding objectively, by appeal to a standard independent of cultural practices, which culture's moral judgments are correct, no do we have any grounds for deciding which culture is morally better, more virtuous, overall. In fact, the very need for those kinds of decisions makes no sense for the cultural relativist in the first place.

We've also seen the problem with intuition or feelings as guides to questions of moral right and wrong: both are notoriously subjective.

One way to argue that people "know" the virtuous thing to do is to claim that they have cultivated moral habits taught to them by their families or culture. After they develop these habits and practice them over time, they come to understand *why* what they're doing is virtuous and will know how to respond as they become involved in new life situations.

This argument presumes, of course, that their family upbringing or culture has taught them what are in fact morally good habits. It's possible, however, that people may learn, early in their lives, practices we think are morally wrong--e.g., prejudicial actions against persons of other races, religions, or ethnic heritage. So, some other criterion must be at work to decide what makes an action virtuous.

Let's look at a couple of examples to illustrate this problem of whether a virtuous person, just because he or she is virtuous, knows the morally right thing to do.

We expect nurses to be compassionate and caring. Consider a case where a patient who is near death and has been "coded" repeatedly, brought back to consciousness after an attack that would be fatal if he or she were not resuscitated. Neither the patient nor his or her family have asked for a "DNR" (do not resuscitate) order; that means that any nurse who discovers that the patient has stopped breathing must initiate resuscitation procedures, i.e., "call a code." It's clear that the resuscitation procedures cause the patient to suffer a lot of pain; it seems irrational to repeat them when everyone knows that the patient is going to die soon. Suppose a nurse passes by the patient's room late one night and sees that the patient has stopped breathing. If he or she is a compassionate nurse, should he or she call a code and inflict more pain on this patient or just walk on by knowing that the patient will die? Or should the virtue of fidelity to the ethics of his or her profession or obedience to the wishes of the patient's family members who want a code called override compassion in this instance?

Suppose a company is bidding on a very large contract it needs to win if it is to survive. Employees, stockholders, and the community in which the company operates will suffer severe economic losses if the company goes out of business. The CEO of the company learns that she can secure the contract by paying a bribe to the people who solicited bids for it. Which virtue should be operative here: honesty in the world of competition where, ideally, everybody is supposed to be on a level playing ground and bids are awarded on the basis of who can deliver the best product for the best price, where it would be unfair to gain a contract that should go to a bidder who offered the best product and wasn't willing to pay a bribe? On the other hand, should loyalty to and compassion for the needs of employees, shareholders, and community override honesty in this case?

Note that if we appeal to *reasons* to support either position in these cases, it looks like we are relying on a standard other than just virtue to make our decision, i.e., appealing to a moral theory or set of moral principles independent of considerations of virtue. In effect, virtue theory by itself doesn't help us resolve conflicts that may arise when we don't know how to tell which virtue should have precedence in a given situation. That's why, it seems to me, we need to have a moral theory that helps us decide first whether an action is morally right or wrong and then allows us to acknowledge that people who perform that action regularly, habitually, in situations where it is called for are virtuous people. That's also why, it seems to me, that the job of moral philosophers is to continue to work at clarifying and developing a theory of morally right action while also giving a well-thought out account of virtue.

What About Aristotle's Doctrine of the Mean?

How does my analysis square with Aristotle's doctrine of the mean? Doesn't the virtue of prudence tell us that since a mean cannot be found in certain actions, that's all we need to decide whether it's the morally right or wrong thing to do so that we don't need some special principle or moral theory to tell us that?

The idea of the mean holds true, I believe, only when it is concerned with an action that is good or at least morally indifferent in itself. It is virtuous because a mean can be found in it. An action is supposed to become vicious only by reason of a deficiency or excess, its failure to conform to the judgment of where the middle way lies. Consistent, however, with what I believe Aristotle thought, in the case of actions where no mean can be found, it's not the lack of a middle way that makes it wrong; reason tells us that there's something about the action itself that precludes ever finding a middle way in it to start with. There must be some other way of deciding that it is morally wrong.

Take eating, for instance. I'm supposed to follow a diet that will help me stay healthy. This admonition can be derived from the principle: "always act to preserve your health." Consistently eating too much or too little could be harmful to my health and would be a morally wrong thing for me to do. Is it wrong, though, because prudence tells me that in a specific case I'm eating too much or too little, that I'm outside the mean, or is it a case of prudence applying the more fundamental principle to act to preserve my health? It seems to me that the "middle way" dictated by prudence serves the need to make a judgment that this specific act of eating too much or too little may be morally wrong because it violates the principle. The principle "act to preserve your health," however, doesn't seem to depend on virtue theory, on the determination of the mean, on what temperate people will do; it stands on its own, it is derived from a moral principle that in turn is derived from some more fundamental moral theory--e.g., natural law, where reason dictates that we must do those actions which tend to preserve our well-being and avoid those that harm it.

I don't think, then, that the morality of what we do can depend solely on the idea of what it is to be virtuous; I believe that a person could do something morally right, morally praiseworthy in a given instance (unless, of course, some unworthy motive is at work) even if, in other circumstances, because of his or her character, he or she would not ordinarily, habitually, do that.

Is Virtue Its Own Reward?

Virtue is often said to be its own reward, not in the way the Stoics thought it was but in the sense that the practice of virtue gives us satisfaction, makes us "happy." As was pointed out earlier, Aristotle thought that the happy life had to be virtuous one.

One meaning of virtue as rewarding might be illustrated by an analogy with athletic skills. Athletes who are proficient at their sport realize a kind of enjoyment, a sense of exhilaration, just in the exercise of the skills to play well. They take pleasure in achieving the end of the game: scoring, and, especially, winning, but there is also great satisfaction in meeting the standards of good play, in manifesting the skills needed to play well or outstandingly well.

Something of the same sort may be said about virtuous activity. The virtuous person "delights in" the very practice of virtue, so to speak, as well as in the satisfaction gained by achieving his or her goals or plans, the "good" he or she want so realize over a lifetime. A virtuous life makes us feel good about ourselves, not in a puritanical or smug sense, but in terms of the joy, the fulfillment, we experience in living it.

Sources

The ideas of the philosophers discussed in these selected chapters are treated in detail in the following primary sources. They may be found in many reprints and in excerpts in many textbooks.

Chapter 3: When Are We Morally Responsible for What We Do?

Aristotle, *Nichomachean Ethics, Book I* in, e.g., trans. J. A. L. Thompson (New York: Penguin Books, 1979).

Chapter 6: Utilitarianism

Aristotle, *Nichomachean Ethics*

Jeremy Bentham, *An Introduction to the Principles of Morals and Legislation* in, e.g., *The Utilitarians* (New York: Doubleday, 1961).

John Stuart Mill, *Utilitarianism* in, e.g., Great Books Foundation (Regnery Press).

An excellent account of the Ford Pinto case may be found in William H. Shaw and Vincent Barry, *Moral Issues in Business,* 7th ed. (Belmont, CA: Wadsworth Publishing Co., 1997).

Chapter 7: Natural Law

Some basic relevant references from Aquinas' theory of natural law may be found in any of many editions, reprints, or excerpts from his *Summa Theologiae,* **I-II,** question 18, articles 1-11; question 90, articles 1-4; question 91, articles 1-6; question 93, articles 1-6; question 94, articles 1-5; and question 95, article 2.

An outstanding elaboration of Aquinas' thought on natural law may be found in John Finnis, *Natural Law and Natural Rights* (Oxford: Clarendon Press, 1993).

Chapter 8: Kant: Pure Practical Reason

The fundamental source of the material discussed here on Kantian moral theory, particularly his first formulation of the categorical imperative, is his *Foundations of the Metaphysics of Morals* in, e.g., Oliver A. Johnston, *Ethics, Selections from Classical and Contemporary Writers*, 4th ed. (New York: Holt, Rinehart & Winston, 1977).

Chapter 10: Virtue

Aristotle, *Nichomachean Ethics, Book I.*

Plato, *The Republic*, in, e.g., *Great Dialogues of Plato*, rev. ed., trans. W. H. D. Rouse (New York: New American Library, 1970).

Resources (Bibliography)

Abelson, Raziel and Marie Friquenon. 1987. *Ethics for Modern Life.* 3d ed. New York: St. Martin's Press.

Albert, Ethel M.; Theodore C. Denise; Sheldon P. Peterfreund. 1988. *Great Traditions in Ethics.* Belmont, CA: Wadsworth Publishing Co.

Barcalow, Emmett. 1994. *Moral Philosophy.* Belmont, CA: Wadsworth Publishing Co.

Bayles, Michael D., ed. 1968. *Contemporary Utilitarianism.* Garden City, NY: Anchor Books, Doubleday & Co. Inc.

Bonevac, D. 1992. *Today's Moral Issues.* Mountain View, CA: Mayfield Publishing Co.

Callahan, Sidney. 1995. *In Good Conscience.* San Francisco: Harper SanFranciso.

Cohen, Warren. 1995. *Ethics in Thought and Action.* New York: Ardsley House, Publishers, Inc.

Cromartie, Michael. 1997. *A Preserving Grace: Protestants, Catholics, and Natural Law.* Grand Rapids: William B. Erdmans Publishing Co.

Curran, Charles; Richard McCormick. 1979. *Readings in Moral Theology No. 1.* New York: Paulist Press.

Edwards, Paul, Sr. ed. 1967. *The Encyclopedia of Philosophy.* New York: MacMillan Publishing Co. and the Free Press.

Finnis, John. 1980. *The Natural Law, Objective Morality, and Vatican II.* In *Principles of Catholic Moral Life.* Edited by William May. Chicago: Franciscan Herald Press.

Glover, Jonathan. 1977. *Causing Death and Saving Lives.* New York: Penguin Books.

Goldberg, D. 1995. *Ethical Theory and Social Issues.* 2d ed. Orlando: Harcourt Brace & Co.

Gonzalves, Michael. 1981. *Fagothey's Right and Reason.* Rev. ed. St. Louis: C. V.Mosby.

Harris, C. E. 1992. *Applying Moral Theories.* 2d ed. Belmont, CA: Wadsworth Publishing Co.

Hayes, Paul J. et al. 1997. *Catholicism & Ethics*. Norwood, MA: C. R. Publications Inc.

John Paul II. 1993. *The Splendor of Truth*. Washington, D.C.: United States Catholic Conference.

_____ 1995. *The Gospel of Life*. Washington, D.C.: United States Catholic Conference.

Luper-Foy, Steven; Curtis Brown. 1992. *The Moral Life*. New York: Harcourt Brace Jovanovich College Publishers.

Lyons, David. 1979. *Rights*. Belmont, CA: Wadsworth Publishing Co.

MacIntyre, Alasdair. 1985. *After Virtue*. 2d ed. Notre Dame: Notre Dame University Press.

May, William. 1980. *The Natural Law and Objective Morality*. In *Principles of Catholic Moral Life*. Edited by William May. Chicago: Franciscan Herald Press.

Martin, Mike W. 1995. *Everyday Morality*. 2d ed. Belmont, CA: Wadsworth Publishing Co.

McCormick, Richard, Paul Ramsey, eds. 1978. *Doing Evil to Achieve Good*. Chicago: Loyola University Press.

Nagel, Thomas. 1983. *Mortal Questions*. New York: Cambridge University Press.

O'Connor, D. 1968. *Aquinas and Natural Law*. London: MacMillan.

Rachels, James. 1993. *Elements of Moral Philosophy*. 2d ed. New York: McGraw- Hill, Inc.

Smart, J. J. C.; Bernard Williams. 1973. *Utilitarianism for and Against*. Cambridge: at the University Press.

Smith, William. 1998. Rev. ed. *Readings in Ethical Issues*. Dubuque: Kendall/Hunt Publishing Co.

Sumner, William Graham. 1979. *Folkways and Mores*. Edited by E. Sagarin. New York: Schocken Books.

Sverdlik, Steven. 1996. "Motive and Rightness," *Ethics,* Vol. 106 No. 2, (1996): 327-349.

Winston, Morton E. 1989. *The Philosophy of Human Rights*. Belmont, CA: Wadsworth Publishing Co.

INDEX

About the Author

Gerald Williams is an adjunct professor philosophy at Seton Hall University and Kean University. He has taught introductory courses in philosophy and courses in moral philosophy, health-care ethics, business ethics, and logic. He has a bachelor's degree in philosophy from the University of St. Thomas Aquinas in Rome, Italy, an M.A. in education from The Catholic University of America, and M.A. and Ph.D. degrees in philosophy from New York University.

Dr. Williams' 33 years in various levels of management positions with the C & P Telephone Co. of W. Va. (now part of Bell Atlantic), A.T. & T. General Departments (pre-1984 break-up), and Bell Communications Research (Bellcore) from which he retired in 1989 plus his degrees in philosophy contribute to his expertise in business ethics. He is the author of *Ethics in Modern Management* published by Quorum Books and of several articles on business ethics, and he has made many presentations on business ethics to corporate managers.

Dr. Williams and his wife, Ann, live in Basking Ridge, New Jersey. They have five children and three grandchildren.